The Globalization of Food

J. Cole

The Globalization of Food

Leonard Plotnicov
Richard Scaglion

University of Pittsburgh

WAVELAND
PRESS, INC.

Prospect Heights, Illinois

For information about this book, write or call:
Waveland Press, Inc.
P.O. Box 400
Prospect Heights, Illinois 60070
847/634-0081
www.waveland.com

Illustrations appearing on pages 20, 54, 74 (repeated on cover), 84, and 104 courtesy of Hunt Institute for Botanical Documentation, Carnegie Mellon University, Pittsburgh, PA.

Printed in the United States of America

7 6 5 4 3 2 1

TABLE OF CONTENTS

INTRODUCTION

Leonard Plotnicov

The globalization of food is not a new process, but one that began centuries ago. In fact, the participants in the 1998 American Anthropological Association Annual Meeting session on the significant consequences of cultivar diffusion came together for this project partly out of a shared interest in the enjoyment of good food, but primarily out of an appreciation of the importance of food in human history. Being anthropologists, the participants have spent time living with people around the world and so are more likely than other social scientists to have experienced a great variety of cuisines. Also, having lived in communities where supermarkets are unknown (and where chickens do not come without feathers, feet, and heads, disarticulated, and wrapped in plastic), anthropologists, like people in rural areas generally, have a keener sense of how food originates (whether its origins are seeds, pieces of tuber, or eggs) and what transformations food undergoes before being eaten. Their subject matter also sensitizes them to the importance of domestication; the efforts to control the means that sustain life. These predilections and interests inform the contributions to this volume devoted to the social and historical consequences following the diffusion of crops or the introduction of previously unknown products of cultivated plants.

The subject of cultivar diffusion has been blessed with several excellent studies, some going back to the early decades of this century (see Mintz, this volume), that address the profound social and historical consequences following the relocation of domesticates. So what (beyond plumbing the bottomless well of knowledge) justifies further investigation? There is no single or conclusive answer to this question. Partly the stimulation to pursue this topic stems from the irritation of knowing that many explanations are incomplete or require adjustment. Partly interest emerges from the fascination of what people can do with domesticates and what domesticates have done to people. At bottom, in the quest for the nature of human nature, there is the appreciation that nothing is more revealing of what is special about humankind than its intimate relationship with what it domesticates. For these reasons and with the expectation that bringing scholars of shared interest together might result in clearer guidance on the directions and steps to take for deeper and firmer understanding, the symposium took place.

It is important to stress that the participants viewed the annual meeting session as a beginning exploratory, and without expectations of making theoretical leaps, but one aspect of the subject brought out by the symposium experience that warrants attention is how rich in unanswered questions and puzzles this domain is. The curious manner by which maize has traveled around the world is illustrative. *Zea mays* is suitable for cultivation in vast areas of the planet, but beyond its New World indigenous areas it is only in Africa that it is ubiquitous and only there that it has become a continent's most important food crop. Although for certain parts of Europe (e.g., Moldova, Romania) dishes of maize have come to represent the national cuisine (in the same way that paprika, derived from New World peppers, symbolizes Hungarian cooking), much of Europe views maize as fit only for the barnyard. Curiously, a similar pattern of use obtains with the Miskito Indians of Honduras, who are surrounded by peoples for whom maize is the principal grain for human consumption. It is not so curious, however, that maize, which is highly nourishing, grows easily, and has a short ripening season, has not fared better competing with other crops. For all its nutritional value, maize is deficient in protein and in certain minerals and vitamins. These shortcomings do not matter much where human dietary requirements are met adequately with other foods, but they matter vitally where supplemental foods do not compensate for the essential nutrients maize lacks.

Thus, for certain research questions, a materialist explanation suffices. To understand where maize was adopted or where its use is limited to fodder, many contextual factors need to be considered. For example, does it serve better for human consumption, as a means of producing animal protein, for making sugar, or for distilling alcohol suitable as a beverage or for the internal combustion engine? This in turn raises more questions that include government subsidies and whether soil nutritional needs are met by crop rotation, intercropping, or chemical spreads.

Under other circumstances, a materialist explanation is beside the point. As people are known to be creatures of habit, it comes as no surprise that culinary preferences die hard. In this volume Roberts reports that the Keiyo farmers of Kenya continue to raise an indigenous crop, millet, along with maize because they regard millet starch as essential for brewing beer, and beer in turn is essential for certain rituals, many ceremonies, and general sociability. Beer could be fermented from other starches available to the Keiyo (like maize or, as do their distant neighbors to the west, the Ganda, bananas), but they stay with millet. The Keiyo reception of introduced cultivars as supplements, rather than replacements, of domesticates already present bears a resemblance to how capsicums as condiments (chili peppers) rapidly spread around the world, often to be deeply incorporated into regional cuisines. Throughout Africa and Asia (but in only a couple of regions in Europe) people readily added capsicums to their pre-existing repertory of pungents, like other kinds of pepper, ginger, garlic, radishes, onions, and mustard. And while some of the essays here demonstrate the value of materialist explanations, others regarding the reception or rejection of introduced domesticates clearly do not. Potatoes and tomatoes were not readily accepted as food crops in Europe, as Brandes argues here, in part because of their resemblance to and symbolic association with things believed to be dangerous and deadly. Regarded ambivalently for the dual qualities of being able to cure and to kill, the names given to these vegetables (see Brandes, this volume) indicate the cultural attitudes surrounding these crops of which Europeans are now so fond.

The case studies in this volume illustrate that the creatures of habit continue to surprise, that people welcome the novel apparently with as much ease as they reject whatever appears to threaten their comfort with the familiar. *Turbinado* (or *panela*) is the locally made form of sugar in the Andean region. To middle-aged and older people it has the quality of time-tested wholesomeness that in the United States is attributed to maple syrup or honey. The essay by Weismantel and Mintz here suggests that turbinado figures in a kind of symbolic food fight, where "old-fashioned" foods become "symbols of resistance to the pressures to assimilate," and other commodities, such as soft drinks, create a "symbolic identification . . . with the foreign . . . and the powerful."

The social consequences of cultivar diffusion also have their counterpart in costs to the physical environment, which in turn vitally affect people. Recall that the American disaster known as the dustbowl, during the 1930s in the Great Plains states, was linked with sowing an introduced crop, wheat. This volume's essays by Roberts and by Dodds provide an appreciation of ecological considerations and indicate by example the importance of a meticulously detailed study for understanding human-environment relations. The studies here also show that if certain cultivating practices abuse and degrade the environment, some domesticates can turn an environment hostile to cultivation into its opposite. Manioc, for example, widely adopted in Africa, in some places there is cultivated by virtue of its unique ability to grow where soils through overuse have been robbed of virtually all nutrients. How sad that under these extreme circumstances cassava (see Frechione here) offers little more than starch for nourishment and extracts for its price of forestalling starvation toxic suffering. A happier instance of food plants serving as rescuers is the potato and sweet potato. At high elevations in tropical and subtropical climates, as in parts of China and the New Guinea Highlands (Scaglion and Hooe, this volume), soils that previously resisted cultivation yielded to the sweet potato and opened vast areas for human habitation. The potato has had comparable success with rocky soils and climates too cold for other crops. In addition, both tubers are highly nutritious and produce abundantly. These crops anticipated the benefits of the modern "Green Revolution" by many centuries, more efficiently, and at far lower costs. They may be expected to gain ground, figuratively and literally, relative to other starches in the near decades.

There seems to be a tendency to regard some diffused cultivars as having the power of an ineluctable historical force to move populations about or to mold people into shapes suitable for economic means or ends. Even when this view is appropriate for some commodities, it nonetheless diminishes the importance of people acting willfully. Paula Brown, in this volume, reports on the Chimbu of the Papua New Guinea Highlands. The Chimbu treat coffee cultivation in a straightforward, pragmatic manner. Coffee to them is not a master but a servant. Its production supplements, but does not replace or detract from, normal subsistence farming. It is for these people an expedient way of acquiring the material wealth that gives them the modernity to which they aspire. Beyond that, they care not a fig for coffee, being equally willing to use any activity as a means of financial success; be it drilling oil, logging timber, or mining guano. When it comes to human agency, simple farmers like the Chimbu demonstrate a rarely rivaled ability to be opportunistic and adventurous in the best capitalist tradition.

Equally entrepreneurial, the Miskito of coastal Honduras and the Keiyo of Kenya make complex calculations in determining with each planting what is the best mix of cultivars (own and adopted). The investment strategies determining which combinations to rely on include weighing the relative advantages of different crop yields, ease of shipment, storage capabilities, and processing costs, and relating these to microecological conditions, available labor, wage employment options, and market fluctuations, and within each of these factors lies a host of additional considerations, including personal food preferences. The way simple farmers address these complex problems compares favorably with the computer-assisted strategies of American farmers.

The resemblance of rational economic behavior for highly capitalized farmers and peasant cultivators does not necessarily extend to Western categories of thinking. Roberts, here, reiterates what other anthropologists have previously pointed out; viz., that a distinction between cash crops and those for domestic consumption is not determined at planting with peasant cultivators, but is a *post hoc* categorization that hinges on exigencies of cash needs, market prices, and other contingencies.

If the farmers of Kenya, Papua New Guinea, and Honduras use rational economics in taking a gamble or hedging their agricultural bets, others show the equally human propensity to be swayed by culturally induced misperceptions, as Brandes illustrates in this volume regarding the European reception given the potato and tomato. In a similar vein, one wonders how knowledgeable and (presumably) well-intentioned colonial officers could induce Samburu to attempt cultivating in areas which the officers knew were suited for little beyond pasturage (Holtzman, this volume). These examples underscore what has long been known; that the manner by which a cultivar is introduced bears little resemblance to how quickly or how well it is adopted.

The speed and strength of reception of an introduced cultivar also seem to be little affected by the direction of its dissemination, whether from the top down or from the bottom up. Coffee and tobacco were introduced to Europe as luxuries and initially met with considerable resistance. Still, it did not take long for these pleasurable indulgences to spread among the elite and then trickle down to the masses. Freeman in this volume points out the opposite direction of dissemination in Hungary with paprika. In Spain this capsicum product was first introduced to the court and spread from there to "gardens everywhere" during the century-and-a-half following the voyages of Columbus. In Hungary, where it was initially slighted by the aristocracy, it took about the same span of time for capsicum, which was introduced by the Ottoman Turks to provision their troops, to emerge as the paprika-defining quality of Hungarian cuisine. If government-sponsored introductions are taken as examples of pressure or enticement from above, then the cases reported in this volume illustrate that such programs can be met with resistance (Samburu) or enthusiasm (Chimbu).

It is clear from the studies in this volume that how people respond to an introduced domesticate depends greatly (albeit not entirely) on the wisdom acquired from experience. The novel cultivar has to demonstrate its worth by its ability to survive (better still, thrive) under the local conditions of soil, climate, pests, and diseases, and by how well it compares (or competes) with the existing crops in regard to labor investments of sowing, weeding, harvesting, and processing for shipment or storage. Storage itself can be a critical variable, not just for how readily a crop can rot in the field, in storage, or while awaiting shipment, but for how well it can remain hidden—out of sight of marauders, raiders, and hungry soldiers—as with potatoes and other tubers that rest safely in the field, buried out of sight.

Three of the essays here raise questions of whether and how they belong in a volume devoted to the spread of cultivated plants. Should they be included? The case studies on tobacco and sugar deal not with the diffusion of a cultivar but with the consequences of its value as a market commodity. Trade in the processed products of sugar cane and the tobacco plant from the sixteenth century onward suggest that the so-called global economy, defined by intercontinental commerce, is hardly of recent origin. The Samburu case is about the consequences of introducing cultivation to a people ideologically opposed to it and fixated on a pastoral economy. As severe as were the consequences of imposing farming where it was despised and ill suited, this case appears to be beyond the scope of relevance. But all three cases are included here because (as Mintz clearly states in the essay concluding this volume) precious analytical value is lost if attention to the spread of cultivars does not include matters of production, consumption, and the social, cultural, and economic contexts that make them or their products desirable or necessary.

PREFACE TO THE ESSAYS

The following remarks briefly describing the essays that inform this volume are intended as an introduction to what lies ahead or, if the metaphor of food serves, a description of the menu.

As widespread as it is and as rapidly as it has diffused in Africa, Roberts observes that maize has not completely replaced native cereals. Well, why should it? Perhaps it takes special conditions for a plant to have overwhelming success, as with manioc in Africa, where nothing else will grow, with the sweet potato in the New Guinea Highlands (and now increasingly in China), or with the potato in Ireland and elsewhere. But in PNG, China, and Ireland there was no choice, either for ecological or political reasons. The Kenya Keiyo farmers have choice and creatively use their options.

Several studies here, including that of the Keiyo, show that government efforts to direct choice or guide farmers' strategies take many forms and their study requires treating factors such as cultural predisposition, colonial political power, market forces, and so on. To these variables should be added the importance of historical chance or accident. In the Keiyo case, it seems that maize would not have taken hold so quickly had there not been an epidemic of millet disease when it was introduced.

The Samburu, reported by Holtzman, present a sad case. For them pastoralism is quintessentially Samburu and to farm is to lose selfhood. Forced into a sedentary existence, they were reluctant pupils under colonial tutelage. The Samburu distaste for cultivation may well stem from a wisdom centuries old declaring that their land was better suited for grazing than for sowing. There are suggestions in Holtzman's essay that the Samburu live in a marginal zone, where slight differences in annual precipitation turn pasturage to semidesert or to arable land. Perhaps in the past Samburu planted crops when conditions permitted, and maybe Samburu history included trading products of the herd for shares of the harvest more frequently than myth admits.

Dodds's study of Miskito cultivation is sensitive to the importance of the environmental consequences following the adoption of new crops, and his impressive use of quantitative data illustrates the value of employing detailed numerical measures in such cases. The heterogeneous origins of the Miskito people of Honduras are an outstanding example of the consequences stemming from the diffusion of domesticates. Their multiracial and polyethnic ancestry is the result of a plantation economy in the Caribbean based on the cultivation of sugar cane using slave labor from Africa. Little wonder they are so culturally different from their neighbors. An interesting feature of their economy is that Miskito men went adventuring as seafarers or warriors, leaving women, children, and invalided males in charge of the domestic economy. This encouraged a reliance on low-labor crops like manioc and bananas/plantains, and suggests that a comparison with other cases where crop choice stems from a shortage of males would be rewarding research. Particularly curious about the Miskito is their restricted use of maize as chicken feed or only eaten roasted on the cob. While there are many similar instances in the Old World of restricting the use of maize (Miracle 1966; Brandes 1992), the Miskito treatment is intriguing because of their proximity to peoples for whom there is no cuisine without it.

The introduction of new crops can be beneficial, in the sense of putting more food in the granary or at least giving people some options with which to better their condition, and it can also result in bitter suffering. The word "plantation" is associated with the abject misery that came with the forced introduction of the potato into Ireland and the agricultural slave labor that persisted in southeastern North America and the Caribbean for more than three centuries. The diffusion of manioc (cassava), Frechione shows, carries a different sinister lesson. When the nutritionally poorest people must fall back on what is perhaps the nutritionally poorest crop possible and (to make matters worse) gradually poison themselves with it, one gapes in awe at the ill humor of fate.

Weismantel and Mintz find that Mintz's (1985) thesis, regarding the key role sugar (along with tea and tobacco) played in creating an urban proletariat for the Industrial Revolution, is repeated in Ecuador, Bolivia, and elsewhere in Latin America in the formation of a rural proletariat. This powerful analytical notion requires greater explication than a brief chapter allows, and can be examined with more care in the monographs of Mintz (1985) and Weismantel (1988). They also are careful to point out that while the mode of analysis has global applicability, it must be used judiciously, as industrialization and social class formation differ from region to region for historical, cultural, and other reasons.

Peppers are puzzling. There probably are more varieties of New World peppers (capsicums) than of any other edible domesticated plant. Does this mean a greater, more intensive interest in them, or has it to do with the intrinsic potential of capsicums to form new varieties? Susan Tax Freeman notes that Europeans had many "plants to add pungency to foods." One question her report answers is of the nature of European interest in capsicums: they were attractive to Europeans initially as condiments. It is puzzling that they found favor rapidly, given the resemblance of pepper plants to others of the nightshade family; tomatoes and potatoes, which had a very different reception. Freeman's essay also stimulates inquiry into the relationship between culinary innovation and the direction in which introduced domesticates become established. Is there a trickle-down effect, wherein novel foods descend from the dining hall to the peasant table, do they rise from the discoveries and artistry of the hungry masses, or is the direction of no matter or little consequence?

Stanley Brandes writes of sexy tomatoes and hot potatoes with charming wit, and suggests that their delayed reception in Europe may be due to, among other things, their resemblance to biblical allegory. The lowly potato and the lofty tomato, he says, became metaphors for what is desired yet forbidden. That which is alluring comes with risk. Of course, this is the quandary of human existence. The history of the suspicious and reserved welcome extended to the potato and tomato is another of the many examples reiterating the point that decisions on what is fit to eat (and by implication, to cultivate) do not rest solely on material considerations. This case study also illustrates that people can change their minds. Put tritely, cultures change. Distrust of potatoes apparently was overcome when peasants, who found them to be superior in many regards to the staples customarily grown, showed their countrymen how well people could thrive on them. Brandes suggests that Europeans first came to accept tomatoes as an ingredient for sauces. Its combination with lettuce and bacon between slices of toast came much later.

The study of the diffusion of tobacco (or, rather, smoking the weed) into New Guinea, by Hays, addresses a problem of reception similar to that of the tomato and potato in Europe. Why is it that the introduction of chemically pleasure-inducing items, like coffee and tobacco, are sometimes readily accepted and at other times rejected, or even forbidden? Tobacco smoking and the plant entered New Guinea initially from Indonesia, but vast areas were without either until European traders and missionaries in the nineteenth century introduced tobacco (imported from America) as a trade item or an inducement to attend church. In some places the natives showed no interest in smoking tobacco and had to be literally schooled in its use. This resulted in addiction; sometimes entire communities were hooked without discrimination for age or sex. Following a suggestion from a publication of Mintz, Hays hypothesizes that where a potentially addictive substance is newly introduced, addiction will precede the establishment of cultural rules governing its use. Hays also appears to say that rules governing the use of addictive substances are bound to follow a period of their experimentation. This is a powerful and intriguing notion that seems to be supported by American Indian use of tobacco and alcohol. Smoking tobacco with them developed over centuries and was restricted to ceremonial occasions, whereas drinking alcohol was introduced by Europeans and quickly resulted in widespread alcoholism. Hays offers a testable hypothesis; that addictive products will be avidly accepted where "there are no models or rules" that restrict their use to nonrecreational (i.e., ceremonial) activities. This stimulates wondering whether the restrictions to one class of stimulants or narcotics can have an effect on other classes. If the American Indians are a model, it seems that these controls are not transferable.

With this planet's areas of habitation shrinking before the tide of human overpopulation, sweet potatoes are a cause for optimism. From Neolithic times onward, the amount of arable land was increased mainly through advances in civil engineering (e.g., irrigation, clearing forests, draining swamps) and agricultural technology (e.g., a deeper plow for grasslands, replacing draft animals with machines). The journey of the sweet potato, reported here by Scaglion and Hooe, indicates that this tuber and the potato (treated earlier by Brandes) accomplish the same results. They can increase the amount of land under cultivation without extraordinary investments in labor and material. That is, these tubers will thrive where other cultivars struggle or fail entirely. What is more, they are rich in nourishment and have high yields. That they also taste good is not to be over-looked.

This volume's concluding study is from an anthropologist, Paula Brown, whose exemplary research among the Chimbu spans 40 years (an exceedingly rare achievement) and covers the introduction and establishment of coffee as a cash crop. The case is of particular interest because the Chimbu do not also consume their product as a household beverage. Growing coffee beans for sale was introduced by Australian colonial administrators and Chimbu embraced the prospect with an aggressive entrepreneurial spirit. A passion to produce and process coffee beans seems to have pervaded the entire society, with almost everyone literally cashing in. What accounts for such enthusiasm uncommon around the world? Is it peculiarly Chimbu? Is it Melanesian? Does it relate to the crop's requirements of planting, harvesting, processing, and marketing, which encourage and reward the involvement of children, women, and men? Yet, for all the profound changes coffee has brought to the Chimbu, they are only partially transformed. The "coffee flush" provides the occasion for "parties and distributions of many kinds, marriages, payments of debts," etc. Unlike the Keiyo of Kenya reported by Roberts, whose expressive occasions depend on traditional beer brewed from traditional millet, the Chimbu expressive occasions hinge on an introduced crop.

It is the hope of all the contributors to this volume that readers will find its essays worthy of their examination and that the diversity of their perspectives and the variety of the empirical conditions surrounding the diffusion of domesticates will encourage the increased attention this topic deserves.

THE INCORPORATION OF MAIZE IN AFRICA

Bruce D. Roberts

This chapter explores maize diffusion in Africa. Grown as both a staple food and cash crop, maize has largely replaced, but not completely supplanted, indigenous cereals. Despite multiple stimuli for maize adoption, Keiyo farmers in Kenya continue to plant sorghum and millet along with maize, thereby preserving biodiversity while also hedging their bets. Additionally, as millet and sorghum are necessary ingredients in brewing homemade beer, it is unlikely that maize will totally displace them.

One of the most astonishing and impressive sights foreign visitors to East Africa experience is the ubiquitousness of maize. "Something that really caught my eye was all the maize growing on the sides of the roads. There's no wasted space in Nairobi," commented one of my American undergraduate students while on a Kenya study program in June 1998.

The crop that originated in the Valley of Mexico approximately 7,000 to 8,000 years ago (Beadle 1979; Wilkes 1989) has now diffused worldwide. Maize was probably introduced to the African continent by Portuguese traders in the sixteenth century. Thereafter, it was mainly confined to trade routes and coastal areas (Acland 1986:124) and maize was a relatively unimportant crop in Africa even as recently as 1900 (Miracle 1966:99). The rapid spread of maize in the twentieth century has fundamentally altered the face of both rural and urban Africa and it is now the continent's most important food crop for both consumers and producers (Byerlee and Eicher 1997:4-5; Byerlee and Heisey 1997:9).

This chapter explores some of the conditions behind, and the ambiguous consequences of, the diffusion of maize across much of tropical Africa. Although widespread, this most important New World crop in Africa has failed to completely displace native cereals for several important reasons that will be explicated with material drawn from field research among Keiyo farmers in Kenya. The essay concludes with a brief consideration of the future of maize in African systems of food production.

DIFFUSION AND ADOPTION OF MAIZE

A large portion of Africa is classified by the Food and Agricultural Organization as being suitable or very suitable for maize production, and this crop accounts for slightly more than 20 per cent of the domestic food production across the continent (Byerlee and Heisey 1997:16). Grown as both a staple food and a cash crop, maize has largely, but not completely, supplanted indigenous African cereals, such as sorghum and millet. The prominence of maize varies by region, with southern and eastern Africa manifesting by far the greatest distribution. In southern Africa, maize is clearly the dominant staple, occupying a position similar to that of rice in southeast Asia. In Malawi, for example, it accounts for over 50 per cent of the calories consumed and 80 per cent of the cultivated area (Byerlee and Heisey 1997:16). Per capita maize consumption in Malawi is as high as 160 kilograms (352 pounds); only in Mexico and Guatemala, where maize originated, do people consume more (Byerlee and Heisey 1997:16). In eastern Africa maize is also the dominant food staple, where it accounts for around 30 per cent of the total caloric consumption. In Kenya maize accounts for about 40 per cent of the total caloric consumption, while per capita consumption is 125 kilograms (275 pounds) (Byerlee and Heisey 1997:16).

The transition to maize production in Kenya began during World War I, when the colonial government encouraged farmers to plant it for the war effort. A simultaneous millet disease epidemic led to famine and, as a result, millet seed stocks were consumed instead of being saved for planting. The colonial government also contributed to the replacement of millet as a staple by maize.

By providing farmers with seed of a late maturing white maize variety, the colonial government sped the transition from a millet- to a maize-based economy. After the war, the development of export markets encouraged maize production, and by the 1930s maize was established as the dominant food crop of much of Kenya. . . . (Byerlee and Heisey 1997:9-10)

Apparently the colonial government in Kenya was extremely forceful in promoting maize adoption.

It did not diffuse; it was "determined" by the colonial administration in the same sense as cotton or coffee. . . . The evidence shows that maize was introduced to many of the people of Kenya by the colonial administration as a cash crop, in much the same sense as cotton in Uganda. (Bowles 1979:200)

Additionally, from the farmer's perspective, there were numerous incentives for adopting maize. Touching on a few here, the advantages of maize over native African grains include decreased labor requirements during cultivation (much easier weeding), easier processing (since there is no threshing or winnowing involved), fewer problems with bird pests, better storage qualities, and greater marketability (Acland 1986; Hassan and Karanja 1997:81). Tastes have also changed. People now prefer porridge (called *ugali* in eastern Africa and *sadza* in southern Africa) made with maize meal, although most Kenyans I know welcome porridge made from millet when it is available. Moreover, as Miracle (1966:4) notes, "[b]ecause immature maize is tasty and relatively easy to eat directly from the cob, maize can be harvested over a long period, being consumed as a vegetable at the first of the season and later as a hard grain." Thus the period during which maize can be consumed, in one form or another, is longer than that for indigenous cereals.

Nonetheless, these assertions do not imply that maize, even hybrid varieties, is better adapted than native cereals to the diverse climatic and edaphic conditions in sub-Saharan Africa. Maize cannot compare with millet and sorghum for their superior abilities to endure heat and drought (Anochili 1984:18-35). Much of the recent expansion in area devoted to maize cultivation has in fact occurred in semiarid regions of east and southern Africa that are not well suited to this crop (Byerlee and Heisey 1997:13). Maize is highly susceptible to waterlogging and it makes extremely heavy demands of the soil for nitrogen (Saka et al. 1994). Moreover, maize

offers poor protection to the soil from direct raindrop impact even when it is mature, let alone when it has just been planted. Soil erosion is usually high under maize unless strong conservation practices are followed. The problem is exacerbated when maize is grown on steep slopes, as is often the case in highland areas. . . . (Lewis and Berry 1988:263)

While it is relatively immune to attacks by birds, maize is highly susceptible to attack by insects such as stalk borers, armyworms, corn leaf aphids, maize weevil, grasshoppers, and locusts, as well as diseases such as rust (*Puccinia sorghi* and *Puccinia polysora*), white leaf blight (caused by the fungus *Helminthosporium turcicum*), and maize streak (Acland 1986:132; Anochili 1984:22). Finally, in nutritional terms, maize is deficient in protein, especially the amino acids tryptophan and lysine, as well as calcium, iron, and niacin, compared to millet and sorghum (Miracle 1966:11). Deficiency of niacin and tryptophan is associated with pellagra.

A solution to some of these problems that has been adopted by many African farmers is to intercrop maize with legumes, especially beans. This practice partly compensates for the lack of protein in maize. Furthermore, beans, as legumes, fix nitrogen from the air, thereby replacing some of this nutrient depleted by maize. Finally, maize stalks support bean vines as they grow. This kind of intercropping, although it accords with the logic uncovered through decades of research on peasant farming (Barlett 1980) has often gone against "the consistent objections of agricultural officials who believe pure stands to be more 'advanced'" (Bowles 1979:203). I shall return to this point in the conclusion.

KEIYO SMALLHOLDER FARMERS

In the area of Kenya where I conducted ethnographic research, Keiyo District of the Rift Valley Province,[1] the Keiyo smallholder farmers understand the mixed attributes of maize cultivation and consequently continue to plant (albeit in restricted quantities) sorghum and millet along with maize. Keiyo District is ecologically heterogeneous and is comprised of three major environmental zones: a highland plateau of 2,000 meters and above (Kalenjin, *mosop*); the hilly, rocky face of the Elgeyo Escarpment, between 1,200 and 2,000 meters (*lagam* or *kurget*); and the Kerio River Valley floor, running from 800 to 1,200 meters in elevation (*soi*). As Table 1 demonstrates, people grow a multiplicity of crops there. Table 2 displays the number of crops grown by households in the locations where this research was conducted. The actual crops grown and the mixture of cultivation with animal husbandry and other subsidiary activities, both on and off farm, vary across ecological zones and also, of course, socioeconomic strata. While maize (*Zea mays*) and beans (*Phaseolus vulgaris*) are the staple food crops of the highlands and escarpment, their cultivation lower in the valley is riskier due to the lower precipitation and scarce surface water there. Even though they are not as widely cultivated today as in the past, finger millet (*Eleusine coracana*), sorghum (*Sorghum vulgare*), and cowpeas (*Vigna unguiculata*) are better adapted to the more arid conditions at these lower elevations (Anochili 1984:40; Kipkorir and Ssenyonga 1985:54-55).

In the highlands and on the escarpment maize and beans serve both as food and cash crops (Little and Horowitz 1987). Additionally, the highlands offer suitable conditions for growing a wide range of cash crops such as pyrethrum (*Chrysanthemum cinerariaefolium*), tomatoes (*Lycopersicon esculentum*), Irish potatoes (*Solanum tuberosum*), cabbage (*Brassica oleracea var. capitata*), kale (*Brassica oleracea var. acephala*), and tree crops such as oranges (*Citrus sinensis*) and coffee (*Coffee arabica*).

Table 3 shows the most common food crops of the three areas.[2] While millet is still grown, it has become secondary to maize and beans. In the highlands millet places third as a food crop behind potatoes, another import. Potatoes do well in the cool temperatures of the highlands, and they also function as a cash crop.

Of course the distinction between "cash" and "food" crops is often an artificial one imposed by the observer (Little and Horowitz 1987). Many people in Keiyo District, like people in other parts of the country, grow crops such as maize both for sale and consumption. People may state production goals for sale and consumption; nonetheless, for most people these numbers will be altered by reality. Emergency needs for cash arise; medical expenses, school fees, funerals, etc. A person who estimates that he or she will harvest twenty bags of maize may originally plan to sell only ten bags this year and store the rest for self-provisioning (food and seed). However, if an emergency arises at harvest time or thereafter, some of the

Table 1: Partial List of Crops Grown in Keiyo District, Kenya

Common Name	Scientific Name
Maize	*Zea mays*
Beans	*Phaseolus vulgaris*
Finger millet	*Eleusine coracana*
Sorghum	*Sorghum vulgare*
Kale	*Brassica oleracea var. acephala*
Cabbage	*Brassica oleracea var. capitata*
Tomato	*Lycopersicon esculentum*
Orange	*Citrus sinensis*
Banana	*Musa sapientum*
Coffee	*Coffee arabica*
Sugar cane	*Saccharum officinarum*
Potato	*Solanum tuberosum*
Pyrethrum	*Chrysanthemum cinerariaefolium*
Papaya	*Carica papaya*
Sweet potato	*Ipomoea batatas*
Cassava	*Manihot esculenta*
Mango	*Mangifera indica*
Pumpkin	*Cucurbita maxima*
Onion	*Allium cepa var. cepa*
Peppers	*Capsicum frutescens* (red), *annum* (sweet)
Cotton	*Gossypium hirsutum*
Tobacco	*Nicotiana tabacum*
Tree tomato	*Cyphomandra betacea*
Peas	*Pisum sativum*
Pineapple	*Ananas comosus*
Passion fruit	*Passiflora edulis*
Groundnuts	*Arachis hypogaea*
Lemon	*Citrus limon*
Avocado	*Persea americana*
Guava	*Psidium guajava*
Carrot	*Daucus carota*
Yam	*Dioscorea alata*
Wheat	*Triticum aestivum*
Cowpea	*Vigna unguiculata*
Gourd	*Lagenaria siceraria*
Napier grass	*Pennisetum purpureum*
Lettuce	*Lactuca sativa*
Pigeon peas	*Cajanus cajan*

Table 2: Number of Crops Grown in Keiyo District

No. of Crops	Highlands Households		Escarpment Households		Valley Households	
	No.	Per cent	No.	Per cent	No.	Per cent
0	1	1.3	1	1.2	1	2.0
1	0	0.0	0	0.0	2	4.0
2	2	2.6	6	7.0	10	20.0
3	1	1.3	18	21.0	22	44.0
4	6	7.8	17	20.0	6	12.0
5	10	13.0	12	14.0	5	10.0
6	10	13.0	9	10.5	1	2.0
7	10	13.0	11	12.8	0	0.0
8	12	15.6	4	4.7	0	0.0
9	11	14.3	3	3.5	1	2.0
10+	14	18.2	5	5.8	2	4.0

	Highlands	Escarpment	Valley
Average no. crops grown	7.4	5.1	3.5
Maximum no. crops grown	14.0	11.0	12.0
Minimum	0	0	0

Table 3: Most Common Food Crops of Keiyo District

	Highlands	Escarpment	Valley
#1 Food crop	Maize	Maize	Maize
#2 Food crop	Beans	Beans	Beans
#3 Food crop	Potatoes	Millet	Millet

Table 4: Most Common Cash Crops of Keiyo District

	Highlands	Escarpment	Valley
#1 Cash crop	Kale	Maize	Maize
#2 Cash crop	Cabbages	Bananas	None
#3 Cash crop	Tomatoes	Beans	None

maize that was originally intended for home consumption will likely end up being sold, often for low prices to local entrepreneurs, such as shop (*duka*) owners. Furthermore, and unfortunately for the individuals involved, they may later have to buy this maize back at inflated prices. Shipton (1990:367) notes that

contrary to some economic assumptions, foods small farmers sell are not necessarily "surpluses." Across Africa, poorer farmers sell crops heavily despite low prices after the current harvest and pay much higher prices to rebuy their equivalent in the hungry season before the next (to economists, a "perverse supply response"). In many areas a few solvent farmers or traders speculate in these seasonal "futures" markets, as something like crop pawnbrokers. When repeated year after year, the process seems to be a poverty ratchet. . . .

As Table 4 illustrates, for people of the escarpment and the valley, crops which are grown for food also tend to be sold for cash. In the highlands, on the other hand, crops that are grown for sale tend to be different from those grown for consumption. Households in the highlands are located in much closer proximity to the daily markets, in towns such as Iten and Eldoret, than are households on the escarpment and in the valley; this strongly influences the crops that people choose to grow. The greater perishability of crops such as kale, cabbages, and tomatoes makes growing and transporti. them from lower elevations riskier and less profitable. On the other hand, maize and beans, once dried, can be stored for relatively long periods of time.

People continue to grow small quantities of millet and sorghum for several reasons. Such practices can and should be interpreted as having the effect of helping to preserve biodiversity, while also permitting farmers to hedge their bets and better ensure economic survival. However, we must guard against the temptation to attribute all behavior to adaptive qualities and/or socioeconomic factors, thereby overlooking the fact that we deal here with *Homo sapiens aestheticus*. As Mintz (1996) has shown, this is a species that is notorious for its proclivity to enjoy good food and drink. In Keiyo District millet is still considered to be an essential ingredient in brewing homemade beer (Harlan 1989:340), called *busaa* throughout much of Kenya. Busaa made without yeast derived from millet sprouts is considered to be of vastly inferior quality. Home-brewed beer is cheap and usually very plentiful, although illegal. Brewing and selling it has come to constitute an important income-generating strategy, especially among women (Roberts, In press). The highly diverse uses of beer by Keiyo are comparable to those identified by anthropologists for other African societies (Netting 1964; Karp 1980; Sangree 1962; Rekdal 1996). These include: propitiary sacrifices to ancestral spirits (*oyik*), weddings, circumcisions, naming ceremonies, bridewealth payments, rewarding neighbors after participation in communal agricultural work parties, and unambiguous pure sociality. Thus, despite its undeniable importance, for myriad reasons, a few of which were discussed here, it is unlikely that maize will ever totally displace indigenous cereals among Africa's farmers. It has, however, come to predominate in many areas of the continent, and that is unlikely to change.

CONCLUSION

Much has been written over the past two decades about Africa's food crisis (Cohen 1988; Hansen and McMillan 1986; Turner, Hyden, and Kates 1993). In their recent book, *Africa's Emerging Maize Revolution,* Byerlee and Eicher (1997) argue that maize offers several distinct advantages for increasing overall and regional food production. They maintain that more is known about maize production, processing, and marketing systems than any other African crop. Furthermore,

the liberalization of maize marketing, now well underway in Africa, aims eventually to move away from the monopoly of government grain boards and restrictions on private trading. . . . In addition, the relaxation of restrictions on grain movement across district and provincial boundaries in Zimbabwe has improved the cost effectiveness of marketing, promoted small-scale processing, and reduced maize prices to consumers—especially to food deficit rural households. (Eicher and Byerlee 1997:259)

NOTES

1.   Field research was conducted in Central Division of what was then Elgeyo-Marakwet District, Republic of Kenya, from February 1991 to February 1992, with research clearance from the Office of the President, Republic of Kenya, Permit # OP 12/001/196/12512. It was assisted by a grant from the Joint Committee on African Studies of the Social Science Research Council and the American Council of Learned Societies with funds provided by the Rockefeller Foundation. Institutional affiliation in Kenya was arranged with the School of Social, Cultural, and Development Studies of Moi University, Eldoret. See Roberts (1993) for details concerning methodology and results, as well as cultural background.
2.   This information is taken from census material. People were asked what their main food and cash crops were, in order of importance. The results reported here in Tables 3 and 4 represent the most frequently named food and cash crops in each ecozone.

THE CULTIVAR AS CIVILIZER:
EUROPEAN AND SAMBURU PERSPECTIVES ON
CULTIVAR DIFFUSION

Jon D. Holtzman

This chapter examines cultivar diffusion as a salient aspect of the twentieth-century history of Samburu pastoralists. In the context of the integration of pastoralists within colonial and independent East African states, cultivars and cultivation are metonymic of broad-ranging issues related to social change. The chapter contrasts European evolutionary discourses on the spread of cultivars with indigenous ones which largely devalue agricultural products, while exploring the conflicting meanings stemming from the emergence of agricultural products as necessary components of everyday life.

At Loibor Nkare, in the Samburu highlands west of Maralal, lives a man in his early to mid-fifties named Lanyaunga Letuaa. He is a Samburu elder of the Lkishilli age set, initiated into manhood around 1960. Like many Samburu elders he has two wives, many children, and a smallish but respectable herd of about twenty cows. His salient oddity is his first name: Lanyaunga, translated roughly as he who eats flour (from the Maa *anya,* to eat, and the Kiswahili *unga,* for flour). The peculiarity of this appellation derives centrally from the apparent necessity to affix to the identity of this man the fact that he undertakes an activity which is so mundane and commonplace. In contemporary Samburu life, after all, who does not eat flour? He might as well be named Lamatnkare (he who drinks water) or a similar term to indicate that he sleeps in a bed, or defecates in the bush, or that he admires cows—like eating flour, all unexceptional activities which any Samburu might do on any day, perhaps every day, and which could scarcely be used to distinguish one Samburu from another.

There is of, course, one important difference between Letuaa's first name and these other hypothetical and nonexistent names, and this is a difference of history. While if in contemporary Samburu life eating agricultural products is as commonplace an activity as drinking water, sleeping in a bed, and the like, this has certainly not always been so. Having historically been among the wealthiest of pastoral peoples (Spencer 1965), with the ability to survive exclusively on the products of their herds a central cultural value (Arhem 1987), Samburu did not practice agriculture, and generally disdained agricultural products, except when drought and famine necessitated that they trade for grain from agricultural neighbors (Sobania 1991). In contrast, it is only a small number of Samburu, generally living in relatively remote areas, who today can hope to even begin to approach this ideal of a purely pastoral diet, with even these doing so only incompletely. Virtually all contemporary Samburu are dependent to a high degree on agricultural products, particularly maize and maize meal, purchased from shops in trading centers, provided as famine relief, or in some cases grown in incipient, small-scale agricultural plots. Inscribed, then, in the identity of Lanyaunga Letuaa is this historical transformation of the Samburu life of his early years—when eating maize meal was of some note, when finely milled European flour was sometimes looked upon with curious disdain for its ash-like qualities—to a contemporary context in which agricultural products are a commonplace, dietary necessity of everyday survival.

This chapter explores some of the historical, cultural, political, and economic facets of the recent diffusion of cultivars to the Samburu. The Samburu present an unusual case. While most examples of domesticate diffusion involve particular crops supplanting or augmenting others, the Samburu case is one in which, as a category, cultivars are perceived to be a nontraditional item; their current importance a salient result of 75 years of encapsulation within a state system. It is interesting to consider in this regard Salaman's (1949) insight of relating cultivar diffusion to relations of economic and political power. Within the relationship of Samburu (as well as other East African pastoralists) to East African states, cultivars have to both colonizer and colonized been metonymic of a host of issues within the process of social change. This essay, then, seeks to examine the ways in which the category of cultivar has been constructed, on the one hand by colonial and independent states engaged in the process of encapsulating and integrating the Samburu, and on the other hand the meanings which this process has had for the Samburu themselves.

THE CATEGORY OF CULTIVAR: LOCAL AND EXTERNAL DISCOURSES

Crops and cultivation have been highly marked categories within discourses concerning East African peoples since quite early in the colonial period. Encountering both agricultural and distinctly pastoral peoples, travelers, missionaries, and administrators drew stark boundaries based on this economic distinction, which became layered not only with economic and ethnic connotations, but with racial and evolutionary ones as well. Pastoral peoples were at once more savage and more conservative than agricultural ones, while at the same time enjoying a racial status more akin to the Caucasian races (e.g., Thomson 1885; Merker 1910; Hanley 1971). If they might be in some way savage, at least they were in the eyes of most observers most certainly savages of the noble variety.

Within the framework of colonialism, this opposition of cultivator and pastoralist was crucial to understanding processes of change. While agriculturalists were seen as quite ready to engage with progress—whether it be through education, missionization, and the like—pastoralists were seen to be uninterested, even disdainful of change, content in the nobility of their traditional ways. In this sense, herders were seen as the inevitable victims of progress, to be swept away in the maelstrom of change: change most prominently seen as the spread of cultivation to their pastoral lands. H. H. Johnston (1886:406-07) writes of the closely related Maasai:

They must turn their spears into spades and their swords into reaping hooks—or starve. . . . Soon there will be no cattle left to raid and the Masai will range the wide deserted plains in all their splendid, insolent bravery and die of inanation. The inhabitants of the walled cities or lofty hills will dwell secure from attack, and the wretched remnants of vanquished tribes still lingering in unprotected haunts will not be worth robbing. Then the proud Masai must turn to and wring from the soil the sustenance which only comes as the reward of honest labor.

Though this was written over a century ago, the images are not distant from contemporary discourses on East African pastoralists.

That the 1987 coffee-table book *The Last of the Maasai* (Amin 1987) could share the title with the colonial administrator Hinde's (1901) *Last of the Masai* speaks not to the resiliency of these last few Maasai, but rather to the resiliency of evolutionary images concerning the pastoral way of life. Into the 1990s, development projects continue to promote cultivation among pastoralists as a necessary, and indeed inevitable step in their integration within East African economies and polities.

This, then, frames one discourse of cultivars prevalent in regard to East African pastoralists, one representing evolutionary progress. Not surprisingly, indigenous discourses present a rather different view. The opposition between cultivars and pastoral foods is a central feature of the cultural values of East African pastoralists, and has been a concern of significant scholarship. A reliance on a pastoral diet of meat, milk, and blood and a general avoidance of cultivated food have long been noted of central importance in constructing the identity of Maa-speaking pastoralists (e.g, Galaty 1982), summarized nicely in the title of Arhem's (1987) *Meat, Milk and Blood: Pastoral Diet as Cultural Code,* emphasizing that while such a diet has never been easy to realize, it forms an important means through which Maa-speakers construct their own identity. Pastoral products are seen to be the only proper foods, and the need to consume other foods (be they cultivars or wild foods) is seen to be a consequence of poverty, of having inadequate herds to sustain themselves on proper food. Substantial discord, then, exists between outside discourses emphasizing the progressive and inevitable spread of cultivars to pastoral regions, and the ways in which Maa-speakers have themselves conceptualized agricultural products.

I turn now to a discussion of the ways in which these discourses come together within the twentieth-century history of the northern-most of the Maa-speakers, the Samburu. More precisely, attention is focused on the cultivation agendas of colonial and postcolonial agents of change and how, conversely, the spread of crops—whether as commodities or in the incipient rise of small-scale horticulture—has been understood by the Samburu as a central means of understanding change.

THE SAMBURU CONTEXT

Space limitations allow presenting only a brief history of cultivation among the Samburu in the context of their twentieth-century encapsulation within colonial and independent East African states. (For a more detailed account, see Holtzman 1996, 1997.) The emphasis here is to examine in a broader sense the ways in which images of farming have informed strategies concerning change, and have been used both by Samburu and external agents in understanding change.

Visits by Europeans to what is now Samburu district began in the late nineteenth century, though there was not a firmly established colonial presence in the area until the 1920s, when a permanent station was established by the British at Barsaloi. At this time the Samburu practiced no agriculture, though they would at times trade with agricultural neighbors for grain in times of need. These included the Dassanetch near Lake Turkana, as well as the Meru and Embu to the south (Sobania 1991; Colony and Protectorate of Kenya 1921). Notably, the colonial authorities were concerned that the trade with the Meru was so intense that the Samburu were going to run out of goats, and on these grounds put an end to that trade.

It is difficult to trace a single, clear external agenda toward cultivar diffusion to the Samburu during the colonial period. This could be attributed largely to the fact, as has been a central theme in recent work on colonialism, that the colonizer did not present a monolithic entity, but was rather a diverse group engaged in sometimes disparate projects. Early white settlers in neighboring Laikipia were certainly more than eager to disparage the pastoral lifestyle of the Samburu as an unproductive use of good lands, but less out of a desire to change them than out of a desire to displace them from the relatively well-watered highlands of the Leroghi Plateau. Colonial administrators took a somewhat different approach, informed both by their attitudes toward the Samburu and by practical exigencies of local administration. These administrators typically express affection for the Samburu under their wardship, as well as limited respect for their customs. While it was deemed practical to enlist *moran* (the Samburu age grade of bachelor/warriors) as corvee labor in road work, in order to occupy their time and divert them from activities like cattle raiding, it was considered inappropriate to feed them in ways which would be contrary to Samburu values. Colonial authorities note in some instances the great care they took in feeding forced laborers only on slaughtered bullocks, rather than on agricultural products (e.g., CPK 1943). If forced labor was fine, forced dietary change was somehow seen as a much more serious matter.

Issues of actual cultivation by the Samburu were similarly complex. Initial colonial plans did include the possibility of transforming the local economy into an agricultural one, and test plots for a variety of crops were planted (CPK 1928). When these experiments went poorly, the authorities became convinced that the land was best suited for pastoral land use and that agriculture should not be encouraged.

Ironically, this in time led to the colonial authorities being put in the position of actually discouraging (or banning) agriculture by eager, "forward-looking" Samburu, in stark contrast to the policies of the independent government. With the large-scale enlistment of Samburu men into the armed forces in World War II, many returning soldiers had a somewhat different perspective on the pastoral lifestyle. Having seen large-scale cultivation in other areas, and having had extensive contact with Africans from agricultural groups, many returning soldiers had ideas about trying their hand at agriculture as a step toward progress. The local authorities took a rather dim view of this (CPK 1947). One suspects that even if the colonial administrators ideally viewed the adoption of cultivation as progress, this was not necessarily viewed as a positive step for their noble and conservative Samburu. This may have been particularly the case in a context in which the "more developed tribes," such as the Kikuyu, were beginning to threaten the institutions of colonialism, and in which any signs that African politicians were trying to "infect" the loyal Samburu were taken very seriously (CPK 1950).

Beyond these ideological aspects, however, there were quite practical reasons for the colonial government's wish to discourage agriculture. First, it felt that the land was simply better suited for pastoralism, that livestock husbandry represented the most sound land use. Perhaps more importantly, however, agriculture would result in the indigenous rather than the colonial control of cultivars. While great efforts were made to integrate the Samburu into the cash economy, there were, in fact, few products which they would willingly buy, and maize meal was among them. Used as a famine food or as a supplement in some areas, cultivars represented one of the very few things for which Samburu would willingly part with livestock. As one colonial administrator noted (CPK 1951), should the Samburu gain independent access to crops through the practice of agriculture, the level of control which colonial authorities could exercise in integrating them into the cash economy would be sharply reduced. Only as it became evident that independence was inevitable did the authorities relent and consider the role of agriculture within local development.

This is not to say, however, that there was widespread Samburu interest in agriculture at that time. Indeed, the policies of independent Kenya toward the Samburu have largely been structured until quite recently by the reluctance of Samburu to seriously consider cultivation. The agendas of both government agencies and NGOs have pushed agriculture as the natural and inevitable path of progress from what they see as a now-moribund pastoral existence. Seeds have been distributed freely, tractors provided at highly subsidized rates, and local government chiefs required to plant demonstration plots even in semidesert areas where there is not the vaguest possibility of success. In some highland areas agriculture has within the past decade or so become fairly well established, including, ironically enough, the area where I met Lanyaunga Letuaa. This has taken the form of both small-scale agriculture by local Samburu, as well as the leasing of large tracts of land to outsiders for commercial wheat farming.

More broadly, however, cultivation remains a highly ambivalent and contentious issue. Events of recent decades have resulted in widespread poverty among (until recently quite wealthy) pastoralists as herds have declined due to a range of factors, and human population has increased several fold. At the same time, increased access to and interest in education have created a younger generation with substantial numbers steeped in ideologies of the evolutionary progress represented by a movement from pastoralism to cultivation. While extant economic problems present an ever-present question concerning the continued viability of pastoralism as a way of life, the civilizing (now perhaps modernizing) cultivar presents a ready-made answer.

These, of course, remain contentious issues. There are many, particularly among the older generations, who see cultivation not as a solution, but as a root cause of contemporary problems, the impetus for spiritual powers to exact punishment on the Samburu through droughts and disease. More common, however (even among uneducated Samburu), is a readiness to try agriculture in response to livestock losses suffered in recent droughts. The logic of this is perhaps less than faultless; agriculture, particularly in the very marginal areas where most Samburu live, is certainly more susceptible to drought than is pastoralism. The readiness of many Samburu to test this path is a product, however, both of desperation in their current economic predicament and of the effectiveness of the dissemination of ideologies of agriculture. In one community meeting between Samburu elders and a German-sponsored NGO in a lowland community, the elders' principal request was that the NGO provide tractors and give them information on what kind of crops could do well in their area, which is in a semidesert region where even grass scarcely grows. In another incident a Samburu elder in a fairly remote area of northern Samburu district told me with some pride of his experimentation with agriculture. He had grown a tomato plant with seeds acquired from a tomato he had purchased at a trading center. "Just one plant?" I asked. "One plant," he replied, "but many fruits." While there are certainly areas of Samburu district in which agriculture is viable, and others where it might reasonably be worth trying, the pull of agriculture must more generally be understood within the ideological meanings it has acquired for the Samburu within the context of twentieth-century colonialism.

The image of the cultivar as a civilizer is not unique to East African pastoralist societies. Gordon (1992) notes the widespread Namibian belief that to tame a bushman you simply need to chain him to a post and force-feed him mielie meal, the infusion of cultivars presumably exacting a transformation of his wild nature. As the Samburu case illustrates, the diffusion of cultivars (whether in production or use) is not simply a natural process, occurring outside social, political, and economic relations, and the ideological constructions of these. Within the context of social change new cultivars and other forms of dietary change may in some cases be more contentious than other types of introduced products and commodities precisely because the importance of food in constructing social identity may be so closely marked by those on both ends of the interaction. If we are what we eat, even more significant is the fact that they are what they eat. Thus an important piece of understanding the process of cultivar diffusion is the way that cultivars—individually or as a category—are themselves constructed in contexts of unequal relations of power.

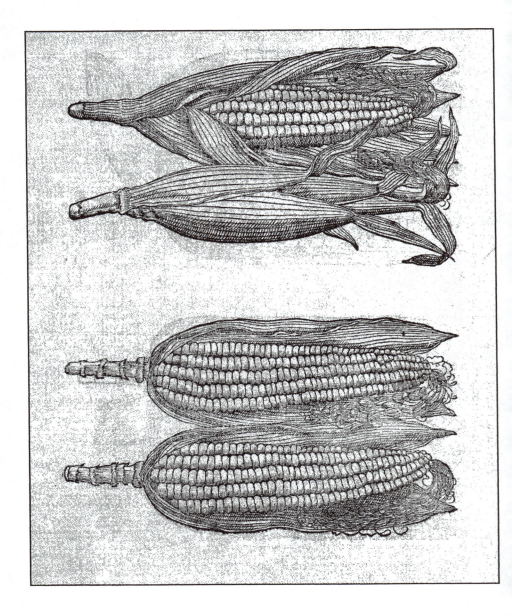

MISKITO FOODS, MISKITO FORESTS: CROP ADOPTION AND THE ALTERATION OF AN INDIGENOUS LANDSCAPE

David J. Dodds

The adoption of Old World crops by New World peoples altered traditional subsistence patterns as well as the indigenous landscape of the Americas. For the Miskito of Honduras, the adoption of rice, bananas, and plantains has had the ecological effect of extensification of land areas under swidden cultivation and more clearing of local forests. However, these crops continue to provide important flexibility within the household economy in terms of commercialization and food security.

The Columbian encounter resulted in great gene flows between Old and New Worlds, especially with regard to crops, domestic animals, diseases, and human admixture (Crosby 1972; Diamond 1997). Many scholars have addressed the dietary and agricultural transformations of crops exchanged. New World crops, such as the potato and maize, heavily altered agriculture in Europe (Salaman 1949; Sauer 1969); maize and cassava changed diets and the agricultural landscape of Africa (Miracle 1966; Roberts, this volume; Jones 1959; Frechione, this volume). Old World crops, like wheat (Crosby 1972:ch. 3; Riebsame 1990), and animals, especially cattle (Rouse 1977; Hecht 1992), transformed agricultural production and huge areas of the New World landscape. As European trade routes extended globally in the sixteenth century, tropical crops diffused more widely and many became the focus of colonial production: examples are sugar cane from New Guinea in Caribbean plantations (Mintz 1985) and cacao from Central America in Indonesian plantations (Geertz 1963).

While scholars have rightly pointed to the vital contribution of native Americans to the global food inventory (Sauer 1950; Manglesdorf et al. 1964; Crosby 1972; Weatherford 1988; Coe 1994), less attention has been paid to the way that Old World crops have altered the diets and landscapes of small-scale, subsistence-based societies of the New World. The question of crop adoption and its effects upon the landscape is especially important in light of recent revisionist research which has questioned the idea that pre-Columbian landscapes of the New World were pristine and untouched by the human activities of its inhabitants (Denevan 1992; Headland 1997). At the time of contact with Europeans the New World was inhabited by a wide variety of indigenous societies varying in population size, density, social complexity, and degree of agricultural intensification (Willey 1966; Sauer 1969:ch. 3). Given this wide range of social complexity, we may assume that New World societies faced different constraints of agricultural production, to which Old World crops offered new possibilities. Adoption of Old World crops likely altered pre-Columbian trends of human impact on the natural environment. What kinds of subsistence problems could adoption of Old World crops solve for New World indigenous peoples? And did this adoption increase or decrease the human impact on local environments?

This chapter's focus is on one society of relatively low social complexity and addresses the way that Old World crops may have altered pre-Columbian agricultural patterns and landscapes for the coastal Miskito of Honduras, among whom I conducted fieldwork in 1991-92. The essay is organized in five sections: first, the introduction; second, a sketch of the origins and lifeways of the Miskito; third, the way that Miskito crops interact with food preferences and contribute to diet; fourth, the relative importance of five principal staple crops and their relationship to forest-clearing patterns; and fifth, a discussion of an alternative cultivar-landscape scenario had the Miskito not adopted their most important Old World crops.

THE MISKITO

The present-day Miskito occupy the sparsely populated littoral of eastern Honduras and Nicaragua. Covered by broadleaf rain forests and pine savannas linked by rivers and inland lagoons, this region has been known historically as the Mosquito Coast or Miskito Coast. Before indigenous American inhabitants of the Coast came into contact with Africans and Europeans, the Miskito as a people, language, and culture did not exist (Helms 1971:16, n.6). The New

World origin of the Miskito (or pre-Miskito) people, however, is thought to be in South America, as evidenced by linguistic, genetic, and general cultural traits.

Linguistically, Miskito belongs to the Misumalpan language stock, most probably the Macro-Chibchan phylum originating in Colombia (Mason 1973 [1940]:75-77, 86). African influence and admixture with the pre-Miskito people, most likely the Bawihka Sumu, is thought to have begun with a shipwrecked slave ship in 1641 near Cabo Gracias a Dios (Conzemius 1929:58), with possible later contributions from escaped slaves and creoles immigrating from Jamaica (Heath 1913:51), plantations in the West Indies, and Spanish mines in the Honduran interior (Helms 1971:16). The Miskito also welcomed intermarriage with Europeans such as English pirates, woodcutters, traders, etc. Evidence from blood antigen tests (ABO, MNNs, V, Diego) shows that the Miskito express characteristics of foreign admixture, especially African, in contrast to the Sumu who show almost no admixture (Matson and Swanson 1963). Ethnologically, general cultural traits of the Miskito show affiliation with lowland tropical forest groups of South America (e.g., swidden agriculture with hunting and fishing, manioc rather than maize as a primary staple, use of hammocks and bark cloth) (Kirchoff 1948; Steward 1948; Steward and Faron 1959; Helms 1971).

The present economy of the Honduran Miskito is a mix of indigenous subsistence activities supplemented by wage labor. At the core of traditional subsistence is swidden (slash-and-burn) agriculture which provides the bulk of dietary calories. Dietary proteins are obtained from a variety of sources including domesticated animals (chickens, cattle, pigs) and occasional fishing and hunting. During the last three centuries, trade goods and money have been obtained by work in various boom-and-bust commercial enterprises such as mahogany cutting, banana plantations, gum gathering, gold panning, and most recently diving for the lobster export industry (Helms 1971; Nietschmann 1973; for lobstering, Dodds 1998). Because of this long-term contact with Euroamerican economies, Helms (1971) has typologized the Miskito as a "purchase society" in which people actively seek participation with the market economy for commercial goods useful to them; when these goods are unavailable people perceive themselves as poor though they still depend largely on traditional subsistence systems for their livelihood.

MISKITO CULTIVARS, FOOD PREFERENCE, AND DIET

In parallel with other evidence for South American origins, the majority of Miskito food crops have origins in the lowland neotropics and Amazonia, rather than Mesoamerica. During my fieldwork in Belen, Honduras, I was able to identify 52 food cultivars used by the Miskito, though this is surely not an exhaustive list. Table 1 summarizes these by crop type and place of origin: 61 per cent are of New World origin, 33 per cent derive from the Old World, and 6 per cent are difficult to determine because of conflicting botanical identification, or because origins are debated by botanists. Table 2 (see Appendix) contains a more complete list of the 52 cultivars by type, common name, species name, and place of origin.

Table 1: Miskito Food Cultivars by Type and Origin

CROP TYPE	New World	Old World	Ambiguous/ Unknown	TOTAL
Root Crops	4	2	—	6
Graminae/ Legumes/ Squash	3	1	—	4
Miscellaneous	2	6	—	8
Tree Crops	18	8	2	28
Semi-Managed (for scarcity/ emergency)	5	—	1	6
TOTAL	32	17	3	52
PER CENT	61%	33%	6%	100%

To understand the Miskito cultivar inventory, Tables 1 and 2 list species by general category. The first category, Root Crops, contains six species. Manioc is the most important to the diet as evidenced by eleven variety names among the Miskito (all but one are sweet varieties). Other useful root crops are malanga (*Colocasia* spp., *Xanthosoma sagittifolium*), sweet potatoes, and yams. The second category is an awkwardly lumped category, Graminae/Legumes/ Squash, in which fall four species; rice, maize, beans, and pumpkin. Of these, rice and beans are most important in the diet. A third category, Miscellaneous, most importantly contains bananas and plantains (note that the Miskito employ eighteen names for varieties), but also seven other plants useful as flavoring or fruit; ginger, sugar cane, red pepper, watermelon, pineapple, and lemon grass. The largest category of cultivars is tree crops (28 species), among which the most important to the diet are breadfruit, coconut, and peach palm. Most (eighteen) of these species are neotropical in origin (e.g., annatto, cashew, nance, etc.). Fruit trees are useful not only for providing dietary diversity and supplementing calories from starchy staples, but also as property markers in old swidden fallows. The Semi-Managed category refers to species which are not necessarily actively cultivated but which often flourish in disturbed areas (e.g., "wild" bananas and yams, *ahsi* root) or which are spared during swidden clearing (corozo palm, yagua palm). These plants are important in times of food scarcity or emergency.

How do the Miskito categorize food, and which foods do they prefer to eat? Patterns of food preference are important because they define what is culturally considered to be good food and to some degree influence decisions about what crops to plant or foodstuffs to purchase. To quantify food preferences, I interviewed ten men and eleven women with a questionnaire employing a 40 per cent pairing of sixteen common foods (for overall method, see Behrens 1986; for ratings by partial pairing, McCormick and Roberts 1952). The foods chosen for the test represent a mixture of origins and uses: flora and fauna indigenous to lowland tropical America and consumed as subsistence foods (manioc, malanga, peach palm fruit, deer, turtle, fish, paca); foods now considered necessary and believed to be

Table 3: Miskito Preference for Sixteen Common Foods by Ethnocategory of Food

	Food	Category Rank	Overall Rank	Category Mean Rating
Upan	(Meat)		(1)	(54.9)
	Deer	1	1	
	Beef	2	2	
	Turtle	3	4	
	Fish (*tuba*)	4	6	
	Chicken	5	8	
	Paca	6	13	
Tama	(Starch)		(2)	(47.8)
	Rice	1	3	
	Beans	2	5	
	Manioc	3	7	
	Malanga*	4	9	
	Plantain	5	10	
	Bread	6	12	
	Maize	7	14	
	Peach Palm	8	15	
Dusma	(Fruit)		(3)	(42.6)
	Pineapple	1	11	
	Orange	2	16	

Note: Interview sample in Waksma, Río Patuca, Honduras, July 1986 (n=21, 10 males, 11 females).

*The Spanish term *malanga* is variously used by the Honduran Miskito to describe *Xanthosoma sagittifolium* or *Colocasia* spp.

indigenous by the Miskito though many are post-Columbian adoptions (plantains, rice, pineapple, orange, chicken, beans, maize); and items often purchased as foodstuffs (rice, beans, bread). Table 3 shows preference by ranking the foods in order of mean rating within each ethnocategory. As groups of food, meats (*upan*) have the highest mean score, followed by starches (*tama*) and fruits (*dusma*). These data validate the emic view of the Miskito: they prefer to eat meat often, though starches are important as well; fruits, however, are enjoyed but not viewed as particularly important. For starchy foods (*tama*), two adopted crops top the list (rice and beans), and these are followed by manioc and malanga (indigenous crops) and plantain (now considered indigenous though introduced to the Americas soon after European contact). Since rice and beans have good cash value in the local economy, and are adopted items in the lowland neotropical crop complex, one might hypothesize that rice and beans would serve only as cash crops rather than food, but this is not the case. It is common for Miskito households to consume and sell their rice and harvests until household stores are depleted; then manioc, plantains, and malanga suffice as relatively enjoyed staples.

Cultivars and preferences are part of the Miskito food story. But what do the Miskito actually eat? I did not collect food consumption data in Belen since I thought this would be too invasive, given the many other inquiries residents of Belen endured during my fieldwork. Research among the coastal Miskito of Nicaragua in Tasbapauni (Nietschmann 1973) and Little Sandy Bay (Cattle 1977) finds variation in the contributions of various economic activities to the Miskito diet, especially for calories. For both communities, swidden agriculture and purchasing combined provide a high proportion of dietary calories (Tasbapauni, 92 per cent; Little Sandy Bay, 84 per cent). However, the two communities differ significantly as to the proportions of calories provided by swidden agriculture versus purchasing. Swidden agriculture provides fully 74 per cent of dietary calories in Tasbapauni, but only 32 per cent in Little Sandy Bay. More than half (52 per cent) of calories in Little Sandy Bay come from purchased foodstuffs. Manioc provides the largest amount (32 per cent) of calories in Tasbapauni, whereas bread provides the largest amount (24 per cent) of calories in Little Sandy Bay. Bread, however, is a significant source of calories in Tasbapauni (18 per cent), and is ranked equally with coconut oil (18 per cent) as the second-largest contributor of calories. In Little Sandy Bay, the second- and third-largest contributors of calories are rice (23 per cent) and purchased sugar (17 per cent). These differences in caloric contribution point to the different reliance on agricultural production and purchasing in the two communities. Caloric contributions to diet in Belen are more similar to Tasbapauni, where a larger proportion of calories is derived from agricultural subsistence foods (manioc, plantains, malanga, etc.) rather than purchased foodstuffs (Dodds 1994:215-24).

CULTIVARS, SWIDDEN CLEARING, AND THE FORESTED LANDSCAPE

Though cultivar inventory, food preference, and diet are important aspects of Miskito human ecology, the impact of Miskito cultivars on the landscape is through swidden agriculture and its principal crops. The Miskito practice swidden-fallow agroforestry similar to many indigenous peoples of the lowland neotropics (Beckerman 1987; Denevan and Padoch 1987). Most Miskito households in Belen keep kitchen gardens, but the majority of crops are grown in fields along the banks of streams and rivers between five and 30 km away from their coastal settlement. The Miskito plant swiddens in areas where rain forest grows (river levees, plains, and piedmonts with dark soils), avoiding savannas and swamps. For the 1991-92 planting seasons approximately 40 per cent of field area was cleared from primary forest, and 60 per cent from previously used agricultural fallows (successional forest). When fields were cleared from fallows, modal fallow time was five years (households interviewed, N=40; Dodds 1994:270-72).

The Miskito of Belen depend on five crops as their principal source of carbohydrates, and these are differently incorporated into the swidden system. Table 4 compares the rankings of these five crops along various dimensions; taste preference, the percentage of households maintaining active fields, the total land area under cultivation, the area planted during the 1991-92 seasons, and the area of primary forest cleared during the 1991-92 planting season. Crops are listed in Table 4 by order of taste preference; rice, beans, manioc, plantains and bananas, and maize (column A). However, this order is not necessarily reflected by planting patterns. Below I discuss the crops in three groups: (1) manioc and plantains/bananas, (2) rice and beans, and (3) maize.

Manioc and Plantains/Bananas

Though rice may be most preferred by taste (column A), manioc and plantain/banana varieties are the most common of the five primary crops maintained by households; 93 per cent have manioc, 90 per cent have plantains and bananas (column B). In terms of land area under cultivation by the village of Belen, fully 85.5 per cent is devoted to manioc and plantains/bananas (30.6 per cent and 54.9 per cent respectively, column C). These planting patterns reflect the importance of plantains and manioc for dietary security and as buffers against fluctuation in other food staples. Manioc grows well across a wide variety of soil types (coastal sand ridges, river levees, hillsides) and is especially resistant to pests such as leaf cutter ants. Plantains and bananas require relatively low labor once a plot is well established. Both manioc and plantains are advantageous because they can produce year-round: manioc, by harvesting tubers as needed and replanting the stems to grow new tubers; bananas, by staggering planting of stems so that racemes mature throughout the year. Here it is important to mention planting characteristics of manioc and plantains/bananas. A well-tended manioc field can produce for two years, so it must be planted approximately every two years (68 per cent of households planted manioc in 1991-92), thus its first rank by area planted in 1991-92 (41.9 per cent, column D). Though plantains/ bananas are first in total area under cultivation (column C) and second in household prevalence (column B), they are in fourth rank for area planted in 1991-92 (8.2 per cent, column D); this is because a plantain/banana plot which is frequently weeded and harvested can produce for up to fifteen years and so need not be planted every year. What effect do these two crops have on the forest? Manioc is ranked

Table 4: Ranking of Five Miskito Staple Crops by Various Criteria, Belen, Honduras, 1991-1992

RANKING CRITERIA

CROP	(A) Taste Preference	(B) Per cent Households with Active Fields (1992)	(C) Total Area under Cultivation (1992)	(D) Total Area Planted in 1991-92 Planting Seasons	(E) Primary Forest Cleared in 1991-92 Planting Seasons
Rice	1	3 (35%)	3 (10.4%)	2 (32.3%)	1 (44.8%)
Beans	2	5 (3%)	5 (0.3%)	5 (7.6%)	5 (1.9%)
Manioc	3	1 (93%)	2 (30.6%)	1 (41.9%)	2 (36.1%)
Plantains & Bananas	4	2 (90%)	1 (54.9%)	4 (8.2%)	3 (12.7%)
Maize	5	4 (23%)	4 (3.8%)	3 (9.9%)	4 (4.5%)
Measurement Unit	Adults interviewed	Households interviewed	Hectares [Plots]	Hectares [Plots]	Hectares [Plots]
N	21	40	43.0727 [159]	27.8196 [122]	9.7244 of 27.8196=35.0% of total planting area [37 of 122=30.3% of total planted plots]
Source	Dodds 1994: Table 6.2	Dodds 1994: Fig 7.2	Household Agricultural Census	Household Agricultural Census	Household Agricultural Census

second in clearing of primary forest (36.1 per cent); plantains/bananas occupy fourth rank (15.9 per cent); and together manioc and plantains/bananas account for 48.8 per cent of new clearing from primary forest.

Rice and Beans

Rice and beans are ranked first and second by taste preference (column A). Rice is ranked third in household prevalence (column B), third in total area under cultivation (column C), and second in area planted in the 1991-92 seasons. Only 35 per cent of Belen households plant rice (column B), which is curious given its high taste preference. This is because rice requires the most labor of any single Miskito crop; clearing of (typically) primary forest, planting, heavy and careful weeding, cutting, threshing, and drying. Thus a household growing rice must have enough laborers (or obligations which can be called in through *pana pana* reciprocal labor exchange) to produce it. Also, since 80 per cent of households have some kind of monetary income from lobster diving, many households buy rice (and beans) from ladino farmers from the neighboring Río Sico watershed. Most important, rice is the single largest contributor to primary forest clearing (44.8 per cent, column E), though it only covers 10.4 per cent of total area under cultivation (column C). The Miskito state that rice needs "strong" soil which is most often found in dark soils, or low-lying areas (Spanish *bajo*, Miskito *bahlal*) within the rain forest. Also, planting rice in a new plot cleared from primary forest diminishes weeding labor since weeds are often established in soils of old successional plots.

Despite the second rank of beans by taste (column A), beans are ranked fifth in all other categories (columns B, C, D, E). Though beans covered less than 1 per cent of total lands cultivated (column C), they accounted for 7.6 per cent of area planted in 1991-92 (column D). Among the Miskito staples, beans are the most fickle to cultivate; they are easily damaged by insect pests and are sensitive to too little or too much rain (they are grown during the dry season). However, beans contribute very little to primary forest clearing (1.9 per cent, column E); often they are intercropped with manioc or other longer-term crops. Similar to rice, beans are a commonly purchased item when cash is available in the household.

Maize

Maize is ranked last among the five crops by taste (column A). Though the Miskito will sometimes eat maize as a snack (by roasting ears in husks over coals), it is most used as chicken feed. Maize is ranked fourth by household prevalence (column B), total area under cultivation (column C), and impact on primary forest cleared (column E). Though households may sometimes exchange maize, it is much less frequently sold than rice and beans in the existing market of coastal villages. The low ranking by the Miskito of maize also fits a general pattern of Amazonian, rather than Mesoamerican, orientation in food preference.

The crop rankings along various dimensions (Table 4, columns A-E) tell a cohesive story: manioc and plantains offer food security; rice and beans offer good taste and cash value; and maize is a residual to household subsistence. Yet rice and manioc have the greatest impact on the landscape through forest-clearing patterns: rice because of its high taste preference, commercial value, and need for weedless soil; manioc because of its usefulness as a predictable, secure food staple, and its relatively high taste preference among starchy *tama* foods.

DISCUSSION: AN ALTERNATIVE CULTIVAR-LANDSCAPE SCENARIO

I posed two questions at the start of this chapter: What kinds of subsistence problems could adoption of Old World crops solve for New World peoples? And did this adoption increase or decrease human impact on local environments? I limit my comments to plantains and rice since these are the two most significant Old World crops affecting the Miskito landscape, together accounting for 65 per cent of total area under cultivation and 58 per cent of primary forest clearing (Table 4, columns C and E). First, why were these crops adopted?

Plantains and Bananas

Given the history of the Miskito as an expanding population whose men spent time away at sea or made war on neighboring indigenous groups (Helms 1971), plantains and bananas were likely an important low-labor complement to the dependable and low-labor varieties of sweet manioc already cultivated. In a review of indigenous subsistence patterns among sixteen Amazonian societies, Beckerman (1993:417) observes: "It is notable that, in whatever zone they are cultivated, *Musa* spp. give yields per unit area that are significantly lower than the yields of manioc. . . . On the other hand, *Musa* appears to be considerably less demanding of male agricultural labor than manioc." Bananas, and probably plantains, originated in southeast Asia and were disseminated to the New World via Africa, arriving from the Canary Islands to Santo Domingo in 1516 (Smith et al. 1992:273). By 1699, the Miskito had been observed cultivating and eating plantains and bananas (W. 1732:293). However, by this date, the Miskito (or pre-Miskito) people may have had plantains and bananas for over a hundred years, since *Musa* spp. had spread widely throughout the lowland neotropics by the late sixteenth century (Sauer 1950:527). A nineteenth-century Englishman resident on the Honduran Miskito Coast (only kilometers away from my 1991-92 research site) describes "thousands of banana trees growing spontaneously, the fruit of which is so much sought after by the natives, who come from very distant parts to Black River, to gather it" (Young 1971 [1847]: 95). Thus *Musa* spp. have had a long, useful presence among the Miskito for at least 300, and possibly 400 years.

Rice

The usefulness of rice lies in the purchase-society complex of the Miskito. Mary Helms (1971:139) notes: "[R]ice and beans [are conceptualized] mainly as instruments for obtaining cash or foreign goods rather than as food. . . . Rice and beans are called English food . . . indicating that they do not consider them entirely part of Miskito culture." The first mention of rice on the Coast appears in 1780, and the first clear description of rice growing by the Miskito appears in the 1820s (Helms 1971:134). Rice cultivation was promoted by Moravian missionaries beginning in the 1860s. However, extensive use of rice by the Miskito seems to have really started in the 1920s, and commercial sale of rice may only have begun in the 1940s with the appearance of gold mines and lumber camps in Nicaragua. Through time, rice (and beans) have become more important to the Miskito diet and palate, though they were initially grown primarily for sale.

What would the Miskito landscape be like today if plantains and rice had not been adopted? Without plantains and rice, it is likely that the Miskito would have depended more intensively on sweet manioc—from which some Amazonian groups derive 90 per cent of dietary calories (Beckerman 1987:59). Manioc cultivation produces a mode of twenty (range seven to 37) kilocalories per hectare per year in contrast to bananas at a range of 2.5 to 4.3 kcal/ha/yr (Beckerman 1993:81). Miskito rice fields produce about 5.9 kcal/ha/yr (estimating from Nietschmann 1973:147). Thus, by unit area of land, manioc is about five times more productive than plantains or bananas, and about three times more productive than rice. If pre-Columbian ancestors of the Miskito depended on manioc as their primary staple, they would have had a smaller effect on primary forest than do the modern Miskito and would have needed only approximately one-half of their present agricultural land area. This may be calculated as follows:

a. Assuming that the total of lands under cultivation in Belen provides adequate kilocalories for the local population, the sum of proportions of land allocated to the five staple crops is 1.0=0.104 (rice)+0.003 (beans)+0.306 (manioc)+0.549 (plantains/bananas) +0.038 (maize) (proportions derived from per cent values in Table 4, column C).

b. Assuming that manioc is three times as productive as rice and five times productive as plantains and bananas per unit area of land, the allocation of land, if planted in manioc, would become: 0.104 (1/3 manioc)+0.003 (beans)+0.306 (manioc)+0.549 (1/5 manioc)+ 0.038 (maize).

c. Collecting terms, the formula reduces to 0.451 (manioc)+0.003 (beans)+0.038 (maize)=0.492 of total land area as currently planted. In other words, if the more productive manioc replaced rice and plantains/bananas, only 49.2 per cent of the present land area under cultivation would be required to produce the same amount of kilocalories. Of course, present-day Miskito wage income is used to purchase some foodstuffs, thus decreasing land area cultivated and cleared from primary forest (Dodds 1998); so under less market-integrated conditions the Miskito would likely plant more subsistence crops and the figure of 49.2 per cent of present land area would need to be increased to offset for lack of purchased foods.

To conclude, Old World crops adopted by the Miskito have had the ecological effect of land extensification and increased forest clearing within the swidden system, while at the same time providing important flexibility in the household economy with regard to food security and commercialization. A materialist viewpoint is useful for understanding the adoption and maintenance of Miskito food cultivars; soil quality and availability, resistance to pests, labor requirements and productivity, storability, and cash value are critical factors in the calculus of Miskito crop use. Yet the real point of this story is that foods and cultivars are firmly embedded within ideational systems of likes and preferences, the household economy and its provision for subsistence and market, and the historical interactions of local and distant peoples through migration, trade, and even warfare—all of which influence humankind's effect upon the natural environment.

APPENDIX

Table 2: Miskito Cultivars

This table lists many of the food cultivars of the Miskito. Genus and species identifications were made with the aid of the following sources: Conzemius (1932), Marx and Heath (1983), Nietschmann (1973), Purseglove (1968, 1972), Menno Van Hulst (Moravian agronomist, 1986 personal files), Williams (1981), and Nelson Sutherland (1986, Anexo II). Identification of place of origin was made with other references listed below.

Origin References (NW=New World, OW=Old World):

FAO1 = FAO 1989a
FAO2 = FAO 1989b
Mintz = Mintz 1985
PP = Piperno and Pearsall 1998
SWPT = Smith, Williams, Plucknett, and Talbot 1992
Stone = Stone 1984

Table 2: Miskito Cultivars

English	Spanish	Miskito	Scientific Name/Family	Origin (Reference)
ROOT CROPS				
1. manioc	yuca	yauhra	*Manihot esculenta*/ Euphorbiaceae	NW=South America (PP 123-24)
(manioc varieties)		ahlal, Bajo Aguán, blanca, cuatro pie, ina, meriki, mina siksa, sikiski, sutra, tegus, yuca pan (may include overlapping terms). All varieties are sweet manioc, except sikiski. Varieties reported as native to Miskito: ahlal, sutra.		
2. sweet potato	camote	tawa	*Ipomoea batatas*/ Convolvulaceae	NW=probably northern South America or Central America (PP 127)
3. yam	ñame	yami, yamus	*Dioscorea* spp./Dioscoreaceae	NW=northern South America (PP 117)
4. cocoyam, tannia	malanga	duswa	*Xanthosoma sagittifolium*/ Araceae	NW=South America (León in Stone 170)
5. taro, dasheen	malanga	kalin, dasin	*Colocasia esculenta*/Araceae	OW=Southeast Asia (FAO1 34) (PP 116)
6. taro, eddoe	malanga	duku	*Colocasia antiquorum*/Araceae	OW=Southeast Asia (FAO1 34)

Table 2: Miskito Cultivars

English	Spanish	Miskito	Scientific Name/Family	Origin (Reference)
GRAMINAE/LEGUMES/ SQUASH				
7. rice	arroz	rais	*Oryza sativa*/Gramineae	OW = Asia
8. maize	maiz	aya	*Zea mays*/Gramineae	NW = southern Mexico (PP 159)
9. beans	frijol	bins	*Phaseolus vulgaris*/Erythrina	NW = Mesoamerica and Andes (PP 135)
10. pumpkin	ayote	iwa, uhrang	*Cucurbita pepo*/Cucurbitaceae	NW (PP 142)
MISCELLANEOUS				
11. plantain	plátano	platu	*Musa* spp./Musaceae	OW = Southeast Asia, to Africa, to Canary Islands in 1500, to Santo Domingo 1516 (SWPT 269-73)
12. banana (general)	guineo, mínimo	siksa	*Musa* spp./Musaceae	OW = see plaintain above
(banana variety)	dátil	bákara	*Musa* sp./Musaceae	
(banana variety)	filipina	pilipita	*Musa* sp./Musaceae	
(banana variety)	chata	plas	*Musa* sp./Musaceae	

Table 2: Miskito Cultivars

English	Spanish	Miskito	Scientific Name/Family	Origin (Reference)
12. (banana varieties, misc.)		ahlawat, bákara, corozo, cubano, dátil, finga, gigante, kuhtu, pilipita, plas, siksa ihwa, siksa pauhni, siksa prangks, siksa siakni, siksa wail, rihine, risku, tirirís (may include overlapping terms)		
13. ginger	gengibre	sinsa	*Zingiber officinale*/Zingiberaceae	OW = Asia?
14. sugar cane	caña de azucar	kayu	*Saccharum officinarum*/Gramineae	OW = New Guinea (Mintz 19)
15. red pepper	chile	kuma	*Capsicum annuum*/Solanaceae	NW = Middle America (PP 153) (Pickersgill in Stone 112)
16. watermelon	sandía	raipisa	*Citrullus lanatus*/Cucurbitaceae	OW = Africa
17. pineapple	piña	pihtu	*Ananas comosus*/Bromeliaceae	NW = southern Brazil (PP 156) (Schultes in Stone 22)
18. lemon grass	zacate limón	ti wahya	*Cymbopogon citratus*/Gramineae	OW = Asia?
TREE CROPS				
19. almond	almendra	almendra	*Terminalia catappa*/Combrataceae	OW = Malaysia, Andaman Islands (SWPT 464)
20. orange	naranja	anris	*Citrus sinensis*/Rutaceae	OW = Asia (SWPT 95)
21. annatto	achiote	aulala, tmaring	*Bixa orellana*/Bixacaceae	NW = southwest Amazon (Schultes in Stone 25)

Table 2: Miskito Cultivars

English	Spanish	Miskito	Scientific Name/Family	Origin (Reference)
22. mombin	jobo	blums, pahara	*Spondias sp.*/Anacardiaceae	NW=lowland neotropics (PP 156)
23. breadfruit	mazapán	bredput	*Artocarpus altilis*/Moraceae	OW=New Guinea or Asia (SWPT 300)
24. granadilla	granadilla	drap	*Passiflora ambigua/* Passifloraceae *Passiflora quadrangularis?*	NW=Nicaragua or tropical America (SWPT 472)
25. (not known)	japil	hapil	—	NW
26. cacao	cacao	kakau	*Theobroma cacao*/Sterculiaceae	NW=Amazonia and Mexico (PP 156) (Schultes in Stone 32)
27. cashew	marañon	kasao	*Anacardium occidentale/* Anacardiaceae	NW=Venezuela or Brazil (PP 156)
28. coconut	coco	koko Varieties: común, pilipita	*Cocos nucifera*/Palmae	OW=Southeast Asia (FAO2 19)
29. nance	nance	krabu	*Byrsonima crassifolia/* Malpighiaceae	NW=Lower Central America to Amazonia (PP 156)
30. mamey	zapote	kuri	*Pouteria mammosum/* Sapotaceae	NW=Central America (PP 156)
31. guayava	guayaba	kwavas, sikra	*Psidium guajava*/Myrtaceae	NW=Neotropics (PP 156)
32. (unknown)	guapinol	laka	*Hymenaea courbaril/* Leguminosae	?
33. lemon	limón	leimus	*Citrus limon*/Rutaceae	OW=Asia (SWPT 95)
34. mango	mango	mango Varieties: anís, chancho, confite, manzana, mechudo	*Mangifera indica/* Anacardiaceae	OW=northeast India (SWPT 80)

Table 2: Miskito Cultivars

English	Spanish	Miskito	Scientific Name/Family	Origin (Reference)
35. roseapple	manzana	manzana	*Eugenia jambos*/Myrtaceae	NW (see Myrtaceae SWPT 471)
36. sapote?	urraku, zapotón	kuramaira	*Pachira aquatica*/Bombacaceae	NW
37. grapefruit	toronja	sadik	*Citrus maxima*/Rutaceae	OW = Asia (SWPT 95)
38. avocado	aguacate	sikia	*Persea american*/Lauraceae *Persea nubigena*	NW = Central America to northern Andes (PP 157)
39. ironwood	tamarindo	slim	*Dialium guianense*/ Leguminosae (or *Tamarindus indica*?)	NW? or OW = Sudan (SWPT 469)
40. peach palm	pejibaye	supa Varieties: wauhuni (dry flesh); laya (watery flesh)	*Bactris gasipaes*/ Arecaceae/Palmae (previously *Guilielma gasipaes*)	NW = Lower Central America to South America (PP 156); Western Amazonia (SWPT 472)
41. soursop	guanábana	swarsap	*Annona muricata*/Annonaceae *Annona americana?*	NW = Caribbean, northern South America, Brazil (PP 156) (SWPT 462)
42. lime	—	switlaim	*Citrus aurantifolia*/Rutaceae	OW = northern India (SWPT 475)
43. papaya	papaya	twas	*Carica papaya*/Caricaceae	NW = Caribbean coast, Central America (PP 156); northwestern South America (Prance in Stone 94)
44. Am. oil palm	corozo, yolilla	uhum	*Elaeis oleferia*/Arecaceae/ Palmae	NW = Lower Central America to South America (PP 156)
45. coyole	coyol, vino	wain	*Acrocomia mexicana*/ Arecaceae/Palmae	NW = Central America (PP 156)
46. sea grape	uba del mar	waham	*Coccoloba uvifera*	NW

David J. Dodds

Table 2: Miskito Cultivars

English	Spanish	Miskito	Scientific Name/Family	Origin (Reference)
EMERGENCY PLANT FOODS				
47. "wild" banana variety	–	kuhtu	*Musa* sp./Musaceae	NW? OW?
48. (unknown)	piñuela	ahsi	*Bromelia pinguin*/Bromeliae?	NW
49. yam	ñame blanco	uhsi, yami, yamus	*Dioscorea* sp./Dioscoreaceae Use: root as food	NW = probably American tropics (PP 117)
50. palm	–	pinsak	–/Palmae Use: palm heart as food	NW
51. palm	corozo, cohune	sliku	*Attalea cohune*/Palmae Use: palm heart and fruit as food	NW
52. palm	yagua	wauh, waung	*Roystonea oleracea*/Palmae Use: palm heart as food	NW

THE ROOT AND THE PROBLEM: CASSAVA TOXICITY AND DIFFUSION TO AFRICA

John Frechione

Cassava was domesticated in the New World tropics and because of its reliability, high yields, and ease of cultivation spread to central Africa by the mid-1500s. However, cassava is toxic and a causal relationship between the consumption of processed cassava products and the occurrence of endemic goitre and cretinism has been identified in Africa. It is suggested that these health problems are related to inadequacies in processing the roots and to dietary limitations. It is proposed that a similar situation may develop in Amazonia as the region undergoes processes of modernization.

Cassava[1] (*Manihot esculenta Crantz*) was domesticated in the neotropical lowlands before 3000 B.C. (Jackson 1993:323), by which time it formed part of a cultivar complex in agricultural systems in Amazonia (Lathrap 1970:48-67). Currently, it is a staple for about 500 million people, most of whom are small-scale farmers living in risk-prone environments in the tropics worldwide, and is the fourth most important source of food energy in the region (Cock 1985). Its worldwide popularity is based on its high yield per area (both in terms of weight and calories), its ease of cultivation in terms of labor input relative to caloric output,[2] its resistance to drought, pests, and diseases, and its ability to produce even in the poorest soils of the tropics. The major disadvantage of cassava is its toxicity, which ranges from relatively harmless in some varieties to life-threatening in others. The more toxic varieties require an elaborate, time-consuming, and labor-intensive system to reduce the degree of toxicity to sublethal levels and to yield consumable and storable foods.

DIFFUSION TO AFRICA

Cassava was one of the first New World cultivars to attract the attention of Europeans and quickly assumed an important economic role for them. Columbus recorded the existence of "bread" made from cassava during his first voyage to the Caribbean in 1492 (Sauer 1992:54) and by about 1496 the Spaniards on Hispaniola had made cassava bread a regular part of their diet (Sauer 1992:98). Cassava's diffusion to the Old World is intimately linked with the African slave trade. Cassava-based foods, manufactured in the neotropics, were used to provide a secure source of nourishment for the Africans making the voyage to the New World. However, cassava was actually introduced to Africa by the Portuguese and not the Spanish. The Portuguese had arrived at the mouth of the Congo River in 1482 and had made their own direct acquaintance with cassava sometime after 1500 in what is now Brazil. Early evidence for the role of processed cassava products in the slave trade comes from Sir Richard Hawkins, who notes that the cargo of a Portuguese ship that he captured off the coast of South America in 1593 included "meale of cassavi, which the Portingals call Farina de Paw. It serveth for marchandize in Angola, for the Portingals foode in the ship, and to nourish the negroes which they should carry to the river of Plate" (cited in Jones 1959:62).

When cassava was first grown in Africa is not known (see Prinz 1993:340-42 for a succinct overview), but it was being propagated by the Bushongo in the area of the Kasai and Sankuru rivers prior to 1650 and was already an important food in northern Angola by the 1660s (Jones 1959:63). Cassava became a significant dietary staple in certain regions of Africa because of its reliability, high yield, ease of cultivation, and resistance to drought, pests, and diseases. For example, according to a Bushongo legend, when locusts destroyed their harvests during one season, they were saved by their king who taught them how to use cassava, which could not be destroyed by locusts (Jones 1959:64). The traditional foods of the Bushongo before the adoption of cassava were millet, bananas, and yams (Jones 1959:63). Cassava appears to have spread throughout the sub-Saharan tropics of Africa by 1700 (Jackson 1993:321). The expansion and intensification of cassava cultivation in Africa continues today through its promotion by developmental organizations. For example, "Since 1990, FAO figures have consistently shown Nigeria as the world's largest cassava producer—moving from its fourth rank to beat Brazil, Thailand and Zaire" (Babaleye 1996:2). Cassava-based food, in numerous forms, is now a staple for many populations in tropical Africa. It has become especially prevalent in areas of high population density, poor soil, and drought.

CASSAVA TOXICITY

Cassava is "probably the only poisonous staple crop in the world" (Beckerman 1993:420). The exceedingly numerous varieties of cassava (well into the hundreds) fall along a continuum of toxicity that is generally classified from sweet to bitter, as measured by the cyanogenic glucoside content of the tubers in mg/kg (or ppm [parts per million]) fresh weight (FW). Sweet varieties contain less than 100 mg/kg of cyanide; bitter, greater than 100 mg/kg (Dufour 1995:151). To date, the most toxic roots tested contain upwards of 531 mg/kg and are utilized by Tukanoan Amerindians in the Vaupes River region of Colombia (Dufour 1995:151). Sweet varieties of cassava can be consumed simply after peeling and then boiling or roasting. Bitter varieties require complex processing that, when executed properly, renders the resulting food products relatively harmless.

All cassava varieties contain the cyanogenic glucoside linamarin (as well as a small amount of another cyanogenic glucoside, lotaustralin) and the enzyme linamarase (or linase). When linamarin (bound cyanide) and linamarase come into contact through the rupturing of the tuber (from peeling, grating, grinding, pounding, or any process that ruptures the cell walls), hydrolysis occurs, yielding cyanohydrins (which decompose to release hydrogen cyanide [also referred to as HCN, prussic acid, or free cyanide]) as well as the glucoside. It is the hydrogen cyanide (HCN) that is poisonous. Acute lethal doses of HCN begin at 60 to 160 ppm. Both the liberated HCN and glucoside are water soluble. HCN can most effectively be removed by washing the grated tubers and by application of heat. However, as Dufour (1995:157) emphasizes, "although the application of heat will volatize HCN, it usually stops hydrolysis because the enzyme linamarase is deactivated at 72°C. Therefore, if heat is applied before hydrolysis has been completed, the food can retain significant amounts of bound cyanide [linamarin], which is thermally stable up to 150°C."[3] When processing bitter varieties of cassava, it is crucial to ensure the most complete hydrolysis of the cyanogenic glucoside (linamarin) and then the elimination of the resulting HCN, which is much easier to purge than is the cyanogenic glucoside (bound cyanide). Arresting hydrolysis of the linamarin during the processing (for example, by deactivating the linamarase at temperatures greater than 72°C) will result in the retention of this bound cyanide in the food products. Whether linamarin itself is toxic is not clear (Dufour 1995:159). However, "[o]nce ingested, these cyanogenic glycosides [linamarin and lotaustralin] are hydrolyzed in the duodenum (in the presence of bile salts) and cyanide (as HCN) is rapidly absorbed from the gastrointestinal tract" (Jackson 1993:322). Therefore, the ingestion of any bound cyanide remaining in processed food products is as potentially dangerous as the remaining HCN in those foods because it also must be detoxified by the body.[4] In sum, effective bitter cassava processing systems result in the maximum hydrolysis of linamarin (and lotaustralin) by ensuring its thorough interaction with linamarase to produce HCN, followed by the elimination of most of this HCN prior to consumption.

Dependence on bitter-cassava-based food products as the primary staple in a dietary regime among relatively self-sufficient and culturally viable indigenous populations in the American neotropics has not produced serious health problems. The same cannot be said for some African populations, where research indicates that such consumption is causative in the development of endemic goitre and cretinism (Ermans et al. 1980).[5] The general explanation for this problem has been to blame the Africans for the inadequacy of their processing techniques, which apparently do not eliminate sufficient amounts of cyanide (both free and bound) and that, when combined with deficiencies in other aspects of their diet, result in these particular diseases.

PROCESSING

Descriptions of cassava processing systems for Africa and Amazonia are numerous (for Africa, see Jones 1959:102-24; Onwueme 1978:145-52; Simons-Gérard et al. 1980:71; for Amazonia, see Dole 1960, 1994; Dufour 1989, 1993, 1995; Hugh-Jones 1979) and will not be dealt with here. The general consensus is that the African systems are less effective in eliminating cyanide. This should be no surprise, given that the American neotropical systems were developed through a long process of coevolution among cassava, agricultural systems, and sociocultural systems in the Amazonian environment. The indigenous neotropical cassava processing systems are complex and sophisticated and exist within the wider context of the socionatural environment of the populations utilizing them.[6] The African cassava processing systems were introduced piecemeal; most likely by individuals who did not fully understand the plant and may not have known that some varieties of cassava they were introducing were highly toxic. Beckerman (1993:421) suggests that even if the neotropical processing systems were understood and had been ably introduced along with the tubers, current socioeconomic factors in tropical Africa (large and rapidly growing populations, land tenure arrangements, cash cropping) make it doubtful that "many subsistence farming African women[7] [would] have the time to employ them." The result is that in some areas of Africa, inefficient cassava processing systems may contribute to particular health problems.

DIET

The problem is actually more complex than just poor processing. In Africa, it appears to be aggravated by dietary limitations. In both the American tropics and Africa, consumers of cassava-based food products ingest various amounts of HCN (as well as bound cyanide [linamarin]). The less efficient the detoxification of the processing system, the higher are the amounts of HCN and bound cyanide ingested through consumption of the food products. Once sublethal doses of cyanide are ingested, "the body's own mechanisms of detoxification . . . ensure the transformation of cyanide into less toxic substances, principally thiocyanate" (Bourdoux et al. 1980b:21-22). This detoxification takes place through metabolic pathways that utilize the enzyme rhodanese and the sulphur-containing amino acids methionine and cystine, found in animal protein. Thus, the more cyanide that an individual ingests, the greater the amount of these amino acids he or she will need for detoxification. For poor populations inhabiting risk-prone environments, increasing animal protein intake is difficult, if not impossible. Moreover, "While high protein intake reduces the toxic effect of hydrocyanic acid on the organism, the development of goitre is enhanced by the thiocyanates generated in the process" (Prinz 1993:343). Studies indicate that thiocyanate significantly inhibits the uptake of iodine by the thyroid and increases its renal excretion, therefore playing a causal role in the development of goitre and cretinism (Delange et al. 1980; Prinz 1993). For populations highly dependent on even well-processed cassava-based foods, protein foods containing adequate amounts of methionine and cystine are as crucial as foods containing sufficient amounts of iodine to offset the inhibition of its uptake by thiocyanate (Simons-Gérard et al. 1980:80).

DISCUSSION

Studies have shown that the effects of the adoption of cassava as a staple food crop by populations in Equatorial Africa is a causative factor in certain health problems when combined with a diet deficient in sulfur-containing amino acids and iodine (Ermans et al. 1980, 1982). This problem has not been identified in Amazonian populations that are highly dependent on the most toxic cassava varieties. One general assumption is that the African processing systems are less effective in eliminating cyanide from cassava-based food products. Very little quantitative data are available to test this assumption. Some preliminary information, presented only to provide an impression, appears in Table 1. The figures in Table 1 indicate that average cyanide content in foods made from two varieties of Amazonian cassava is 11.5 mg/kg; while the average for foods made from an unknown number of African varieties is 13.6 mg/kg. This difference, which is not likely to be representative, is probably not very meaningful biologically (Dufour 1989, personal communication). What may prove to be more significant is the difference between average total cyanide intakes. The very limited data available indicate that Liberian (African) adults ingest almost two times more cyanide (average daily intake at 0.71 mg/kg body weight) (Jackson 1993:326) than do Tukanoan (Amazonian) adults (average daily intake at 0.4 mg/kg) (Dufour 1995:159). Whether the Liberians consume greater quantities of cassava-based foods than Tukanoans (which is unlikely) or that the cyanide content of the foods is actually higher for the Liberians (more likely) is not clear.

Overall, the African populations in question do not always process cassava as efficiently as do the Amazonian populations. Moreover, it is quite probable that intakes of the sulfur-containing amino acids required to detoxify ingested cyanide are not adequate in some of the African populations. On the other hand, for the Tukanoans of Amazonia, Dufour (1995:160) states, "The residual cyanide in food products is low, and the current diet of adults appears to provide adequate quantities of the sulfur-containing amino acids used in the metabolic detoxification of dietary cyanide." Moreover, the relationship is not as simple as being able to continually offset higher cyanide intake loads with higher consumption of sulfur-containing amino acid foods. As noted above, the end result of detoxifying increasing amounts of cyanide is the production of greater amounts of thiocyanate. This functions to reduce the likelihood of cyanide poisoning, but in turn increases the potential for the development of goitre and cretinism. Therefore the solution to this aspect of the problem requires striking a delicate balance.

Another potentially very important, but as yet understudied, aspect of the problem involves possible phenotypical and genotypical differences between Amazonian and African populations related to biocultural adaptations to cassava toxicity. The coevolution of cassava and human populations in Amazonia has been relatively long (over 5,000 years), and human genetic changes may have accompanied this development. Even over the relatively short time that similar coevolution has operated in tropical Africa, some modifications in human phenotypes attributable to cassava consumption have occurred (Jackson 1993). Little investigation into cassava dependence in

Table 1: Comparison of HCN (Free Cyanide) Content of Cassava-Based
Foods for Amazonia and Africa

Amazonia[1]		Africa	
Food	HCN ppm FW	Food	HCN ppm FW
casabe (fresh)	10	fuku[2]	14.2
casabe (ordinary, day 2)	25	chickwangue 1[2]	3.5
casabe (ordinary, day 3)	7	chickwangue 2[3]	6.3 to 17.3
fariña	4	gari[4]	20 to 30
Averages	11.5		13.6

[1]Data for Amazonia are from Dufour (1995:154-55). The casabe figures are averages for processing runs of two different types of cassava. The average total (bound and free) cyanide content of the whole roots is 528 ppm. The preparation of these cassava-based foods is undertaken through a complex system that is considered a model for effective processing. (For details, see Dufour 1989, 1995; Hugh-Jones 1979.)

[2]Data for fuku and chickwangue 1 are from Simons-Gérard et al. (1980:79). Fuku preparation involves peeling, cutting, sun-drying for one to two days, bruising in a mortar with corn, steeping in water for twelve to 24 hours, grilling, and boiling in water; roots are not soaked prior to processing. Chickwangue preparation involves soaking the roots for two to six days, mashing into puree, and simmering to form a paste.

[3]Data for chickwangue 2 are from Prinz (1993:342) for the Kivu and Ubangi regions near the Congo Delta.

[4]Data for gari are from Onwueme (1978:147-48). Gari is the most popular form of cassava-based foods in West Africa. Its preparation involves peeling, washing, grating, dewatering for two to four days, sieving, toasting, and drying. The roots used to prepare gari in this region contain about 400 ppm total cyanide.

Amazonia has taken place, primarily because native Amazonians have proven to be generally healthy.

CONCLUSIONS

A considerable body of scientific evidence indicates that endemic goitre and cretinism are a significant part of the heritage of the adoption of cassava cultivation in tropical Africa.[8] At least part of this health problem seems due to less-than-effective cassava processing. Many cultural anthropologists would conclude that the problem of inefficient cassava processing in some regions of Africa is an excellent illustration of a "partial adoption"—whereby one particular segment or part is extracted from an integrated whole and bounded sociocultural system. Partial adoption frequently has proven to result in negative consequences for target populations. This is undoubtedly true for the piecemeal introduction of cassava processing into Africa, especially during the early period of its adoption. However, the problem is compounded by other factors, including the need to feed growing populations, an increasing dependency on a very reliable (but dangerous) crop like cassava, shrinking resources (such as agricultural land suitable for more nutritious crops and important supplements to the diet from stocks of local flora and fauna), and ever-increasing engagement with the modern market economy. Fundamentally, as Beckerman (1993:421) suggests, one cause of inefficient cassava processing in Africa is that the processors do not have the time to undertake the elaborate and time-consuming process necessary to detoxify the tubers effectively. This results in higher cyanide intakes which, in turn, are exacerbated by the lack of animal protein resources (the major source of methionine and cystine) to transform cyanide to thiocyanate and by the lack of iodine to compensate for the inhibiting effect of thiocyanate on iodine uptake by the thyroid. In general, it is apparent that the cultural, social, and environmental situations in tropical Africa have been quite distinct from those of Amazonia over the 500 years since the introduction of cassava into Africa.

Regrettably, there is the possibility that the current situation in Africa provides a preview of the future for areas of Amazonia where the most toxic varieties of cassava are the dietary staple for many indigenous populations. Basically, it appears that as modernization occurs (including all of the effects of the absorption of relatively isolated, culturally coherent indigenous populations into the global system) traditional concerns are relaxed. Even for the exemplary bitter-cassava-dependent Tukanoans of Amazonia, Dufour (1995:161) notes: "As women's expectations change with acculturation, cassava processing techniques may also change. In more acculturated areas like Mitu, there has been a shift to fariña and a virtual abandonment of casabe and associated products. The quality of the fariña for sale suggests that the traditional long fermentation period is being shortened."

As indigenous populations move away from their traditions, beliefs, and myths that serve as the cultural framework for knowledge about cassava and its processing, they will likely tend to become more careless in processing (see, for example, Grenand 1993). In Amazonia, indigenous populations are generally increasing, becoming more sedentary (Frechione 1990), and engaging in market activities (the latter often involving the sale of processed cassava-based products). This results in changes in agricultural practices, hunting and gathering regimes, diet and, eventually, cassava processing techniques (see Baksh 1995; Dufour 1995:160-61; Grenand 1993). If these changes result in less effective cassava processing and a simplification of a diverse diet that currently provides sufficient protein as well as sulfur-containing amino acids, it is possible that the cassava-related health problems encountered in Africa could surface in Amazonia, thus bringing this case of cultivar diffusion full circle.

NOTES

1. The word cassava is derived from the Taino (people of the Greater Antilles) *casabe*. Another commonly utilized term is manioc. This word is the Anglicized version of the Tupi Indian term *mandioca*, which is still used for the plant and tubers in Brazil. Cassava is the term generally employed in the scientific literature.
2. Sauer (1992:68) notes that this was realized very early on by the Spaniards. He cites Las Casas (who was a commercial grower of cassava in the early 1500s) as saying, "Twenty persons working six hours a day for one month will

make a planting of such conucos [fields] that will provide bread for three thousand persons for two years."

3. In addition, simply storing the grated cassava mass and the liquid yielded from dewatering results in further cyanide loss, although this is relatively slow (Dufour 1989:89).

4. The information presented here on cassava toxicity and chemical processes comes from Bourdoux et al. (1980a, 1980b), Dufour (1995), and Jackson (1993). I thank Drs. Dufour and Jackson for additional clarifications concerning these processes in personal communications. It should be noted nonetheless that the interpretations presented here are those of the author.

5. Consumption of cassava-based foods in crisis situations also has been linked to adverse health complications. Padmaja (1996) states, "In situations where famine or extreme poverty may force a population to eat poorly processed cassava in a diet that is also deficient in nutrients such as protein, the plant's cyanogenic glucosides can lead to poisoning. A classic case was the infantile kwashiorkor epidemic in famine-stricken Biafra in 1968, but there have also been recent examples of spastic paraparesis, or konzo, in drought-stricken regions of Mozambique and Tanzania."

6. For example, among the Yekuana Amerindians of southern Venezuela, where the author has carried out long-term research, cassava production and processing is embedded in a system of myths and rituals that serve to control every aspect of its handling and utilization on a day-to-day basis (Frechione 1982; Guss 1989).

7. In both Amazonia and Africa, women are the primary, and often the only, processors of cassava.

8. Interestingly, this problem has not been noted in other regions of the world where cassava also was enthusiastically adopted, including southern India, Melanesia, Micronesia, and Southeast Asia (Jackson 1993:324). Possibly, this is simply due to lack of detailed investigation.

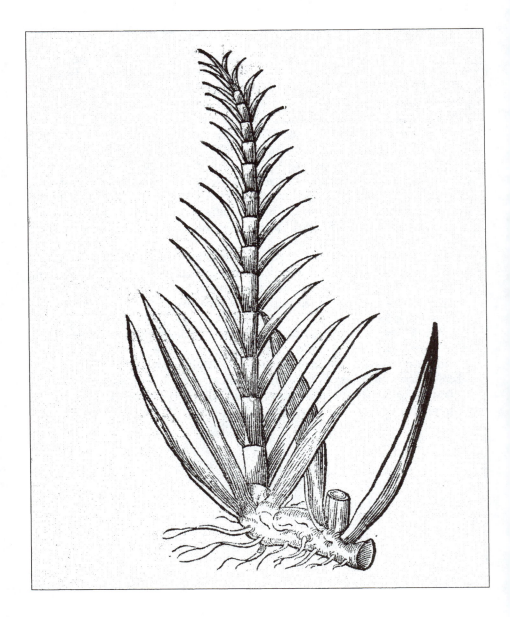

SWEET INTERLOPER

Mary Weismantel
Sidney W. Mintz

Cane sugar is one of the world's most important cultivars; its diffusion involves both global and local histories, in which the plant, the food, and the taste merit separate analysis. Two cases, from urban Bolivia and rural Ecuador, involve various forms of sugars and soft drinks; both cases demonstrate that local consumers are not without agency; but neither can they be seen to enact successful forms of resistance to world economic trends.

The point is obvious, but worth making: a plant, a food, and a taste are wholly different things. Sucrose ($C_{12}H_{22}O_{11}$), still the world's major source of sweetness, is not produced by human beings; it is produced by photosynthesis, and can be extracted from all or nearly all green plants. Its extraction is commercially practicable in the case of some, among them sugar cane (*Saccharum officinarum*) and sugar beet (*Beta vulgaris*). Sucrose is also extracted commercially from the sugar maple, from the so-called Chinese sorghum, and from the sugar palm, among others.

In every case, of course, the extracted substance has a sweet taste; it used to be only in order to capture that taste that the substance was extracted. Depending upon the degree of refining, however, the sweet taste reminds the eater only more or less of the plant from which it was won. When nearly pure, as in the case of granular white sugar, what is eaten tastes only of itself—that is, it is tasteless, except for its sweetness. This has led the enthusiasts who extract and process it to refer to it, when they are at their most ardent, as "bottled sunshine."

It follows that soft-drink manufacturers have done more than anyone else worldwide to promote the idea that happiness is sweetness in a bottle. The unflagging energy of their advertising campaigns, and their global reach, have made Coca-Cola and Pepsi-Cola internationally notorious emblems of corporate neocolonialism. They have been extremely successful in building their markets. The highly publicized entrance of fast-food restaurants such as McDonald's and Pizza Hut into Asia, Africa, Eastern Europe, and Latin America still remains mostly confined to a few outposts located at elite addresses in wealthy, cosmopolitan capital cities. In contrast, American soft drinks, like cigarettes, have become familiar to consumers in isolated rural areas and poor urban neighborhoods throughout the world. Their purchasers seem happy to accept them as symbols of joyous conviviality in just the manner that their makers suggest. However, a closer look at the actual uses of soft drinks, and of sugar more generally, reveals a more complicated story. Within a specific market, this international commodity accumulates regional names, meanings, and uses that make of it a palimpsest within which we can glimpse histories both local and global.

In the Andean region of South America, indigenous consumers are intimately familiar with sugar, and with soft drinks as well. The two indigenous languages with the largest numbers of speakers are Quechua (or Quichua, as it is called in many northern dialects), and Aymara (spoken to the south, primarily in Bolivia). In Ecuador and Peru, Quechua-speakers often call sugar, and most sweet foods such as candy or sweetened hot cereal, by a generic name for sweetness, *mishqui.* But soft drinks, however sweet, are not mishqui: they are referred to by a Spanish loan word, *cola*—or more commonly, *colita,* adding the Spanish diminutive as though to express a sense of friendly intimacy with these industrial products. Aymara–speakers, too, call soft drinks colitas, and both groups have readily integrated cola-drinking into their social lives. In a recently published life history of a Bolivian market woman, Sofía Velásquez (Buechler and Buechler 1996), sugary drinks surface as a mark of sociability and good will between friends, almost as though the vendors of La Paz were emulating the happy, smiling groups of friends in cola advertisements. The intermittent mention of soft drinks, as well as other beverages and sweet foods, in Sofía's narrative offers a series of snapshots of the history and culture of sugar in the Andes. Her story thus provides us with one example of how this curious food has become so thoroughly enmeshed in diet and cuisine around the world. In the changing uses of sugar for the large class of Aymara-speaking women merchants in the capital city of La Paz, we see a local version of a history that has been written in the eating habits of people in cities throughout the Americas.

Sofía was born in 1945. The sweet foods she remembers from her childhood are baked goods and candies: a friend's mother fed her "sweets and chocolates," and the nuns who were her teachers gave her "cookies and sweets" for Christmas (Buechler and Buechler 1996:9-10). Learning to bake was a womanly virtue, and a means of upward social mobility and assimilation as well, through which rural immigrants became more like their new urban neighbors—a process which in the Andes is also understood as a kind of *blanqueamiento,* or racial whitening. The Catholic Church helped in this process, sponsoring classes in which a Belgian woman taught little Aymara girls "how to embroider, sew, knit, and bake little buns, and gave us lectures about becoming a woman" (Buechler and Buechler 1996:10). The priest, too, encouraged the girls' mothers to send their children to catechism classes by periodically sending them home with "ten to twelve pounds of flour and sugar." "This suited my mother just fine," remembers Sofía, "and so she would always urge me to go" (Buechler and Buechler 1996:11).

Sofía's first mention of soft drinks coincides with her adolescence in the 1950s, and marks her first achievement of a degree of independence from older women, whether teachers or relatives. She talks about her friendship with a girl named Lola, who was raised by her mother and a female friend, whom she also called mother. The two women struggled to support themselves and Lola by working as embroiderers. Unlike the British working poor of the nineteenth century, who staved off hunger pangs with tea and sugar, as Mintz (1985:127-29) has described, Lola's parents had recourse to a traditional Andean remedy. "Sometimes they had nothing to eat. Sometimes they would have to content themselves with a little coca. It seemed to me that they were very sad" (Buechler and Buechler 1996:11).

When Lola and Sofía began to earn money for themselves by clandestine market vending, they spent their earnings not on the coca leaf, but on its more cosmopolitan stepchild, cola beverages. Sofía remembers these purchases with great pleasure:

For me it was fun, because Lola and I were free . . . I was no longer tied to my home. I earned good money. I bought ice cream. I bought soft drinks. If someone passed by with food, I bought some and I went to the movies. (Buechler and Buechler 1996:20)

Cash as the road to a form of freedom embodied in movies and soft drinks sounds like a familiar story. Imported consumer goods have often been embraced by the children of immigrants from rural areas to the city as the emblem of their determination to make a way of life unlike that of their parents. But if the story of sugar in the Andes is manifestly global in its broad outlines, it is stubbornly local in its details. It thus reminds us that while poor people in rural areas and cities alike continue to eat more sugar and drink more soft drinks every year, the social events and economic exchanges through which they do so are both like and unlike those envisioned by Madison Avenue. As a market vendor, Sofía earns money and spends it in ways that inextricably tie her into the world economy that Coca-Cola represents, but her chosen profession also requires her to buy and use such consumer items as clothing, jewelry, and soft drinks in unexpected ways.

Sofía prides herself on the financial and social acumen that allowed her to build a successful business in a competitive environment in which most women fail. But the rules of the market in which she operates (the produce markets of La Paz) require quite specific forms of expenditure, and of conspicuous consumption. As a girl, she happily used her spending money on soft drinks, but she also accumulated larger sums, her "capital," which she invested far differently. Embarking upon a career as a full-time market woman required her to expand her volume of sales; and she also decided, as a calculated investment, to begin wearing and stockpiling the expensive handmade traditional clothing and gold jewelry traditionally worn by Andean market women. This garb, which fewer and fewer women can afford, signaled her growing success and thus encouraged new customers to come to her. The first step in this process was to have her front teeth capped in gold, a cosmetic medical procedure that her mother approved of as a sound investment (and so was happy to underwrite).

Soft drinks show up in her story as part of another kind of business strategy. If as a young girl she enjoyed consuming them with a friend as a mark of individual success, as an adult she more often describes them as investments in social relationships, which for Sofía are always linked with commerce. She survives and thrives by building and disassembling networks of friends, allies, partners, customers, and suppliers. The purchase of soft drinks is one means she employs to indicate good will in this constantly shifting world. Drinking soft drinks together thus becomes less an expression of innocent conviviality than a poor man's version of the corporate lunch, a thinly disguised bait offered to a prospective client.

As Sofía grows older, drinking beer with other women, or with men, becomes more common in her story; this activity, although equally convivial, has somewhat different connotations from the consumption of soft drinks. The loss of judgment that can accompany it leads her into some negative consequences, ranging from hangovers to half-remembered sexual acts to involvement in political corruption. Soft drinks appear more innocuous, but this in itself makes them a tool of the seducer, whether financial or sexual.[1] For if the first appearance that soft drinks make in her narrative is when she buys them for herself, their second manifestation is in adolescent tales of young men who buy her soft drinks as a prologue to seduction. It is a surprisingly effective ploy: in the social world of the Andes, to accept food or drink from another is a commitment not easily broken. Part of the problem lies in the nature of the soft drink as such, which so publicly announces itself as a moment of pure sensory enjoyment (unlike a bowl of soup, for instance, which claims to be nourishing, a preparation for work). In accepting a sweet drink purchased by a stranger, one agrees to share a temporary pleasure, a compromising act which may hint at others to follow. For Sofía, the soft drink with a boy often leads back to beer with the girls, for in Sofía's world women are as likely as men to drown their sorrows at the local tavern with their same-sex confidantes.

Soft drinks show up in one more form in her story. As a young girl purchasing soft drinks with her first earnings, she used them to celebrate an achieved status; this purpose re-emerges later in life, when it requires a different and far greater level of expenditure. Her growing success as a vendor leads her into a political career; she begins by holding minor offices in various market women's unions and associations, and ends as a political leader, obliged to sponsor a fiesta for the entire market. Among her many expenditures are those for food, music, masses for the patron saint, flags to decorate the market, and cases of soft drinks. She farms out the latter purchase to a nephew as his contribution to an event which, if successful, confers public acclaim on the entire family. Sofía's rising economic status is reflected in the fact that by this point in her story, soft drinks are a minor purchase, worth recounting only when she buys them for other people. Conspicuous consumption through giving—and especially through the giving of food and drink—is a familiar phenomenon everywhere. But it has a heightened significance and an elaborated set of rituals in the Andes, where older economies based upon the gift have been refashioned into peculiarly indigenous forms of capitalist competition and commodity fetishism. Soft-drink advertising often depicts a group of smiling people, each with a beverage in hand. But this picture can mean different things. Young, middle-class employees at an advertising firm in Manhattan envision an afternoon of egalitarian pleasure shared by independent consumers, each of whom has purchased his or her own bottle of soda. To Andean eyes, such a scene is more likely to signal an event sponsored by a wealthy host; an employer, a union leader, a crew boss, a godmother. In this context, the consumption of a soft drink is a pleasure complicated by obligation and inequality, but also by a deep social bond unlikely to be achieved through similar moments in the United States.

Sofía Velásquez is not a peasant; she inhabits an entirely urban and commercial world. Even when she goes to the countryside, she represents the penetration of urban commerce into the rural sphere; in fact, her mother's store, which sold bottled sodas and beers in a little farm town, was itself the very sign of the city come to the country. When Sofía returns to that community as an adult, she buys farm produce with money that enables farmers to engage in other commercial exchanges. Thus her particular life history, and the role of soft drinks and sugar in it, does not represent all indigenous Andean women of her generation, but the particularities of the urban Aymara experience. Even at that, she is in many ways a remarkable and atypical woman, as the Buechlers (1996:xxvi and passim) are at pains to point out. In her lifetime, the past is represented by that brief period when city women baked cookies and thought themselves modern for doing so; the present is a more commoditized and industrialized world, in which treats take the form of soft drinks and mass-produced cookies and candies. She herself, like most market women, cooks at home only when she prepares foods to sell. She eats her meals and drinks her beers and sodas in restaurants or buys them from other vendors.

Sofía takes soft drinks for granted, but other indigenous women of her generation do not. When Weismantel did fieldwork in the rural Ecuadorian community of Zumbagua in the 1980s, soft drinks still had the kind of cachet of youth and modernity that Velásquez remembers in La Paz in the 1950s. On one occasion, she bought a soda at the Saturday market for a young girl, who was thrilled and sucked it down with great pleasure. Her grandmother was less enthusiastic, commenting suspiciously that she had never tasted a soft drink and did not know why young people would want to drink one. Curious as to whether this world-famous beverage would live up its claim of universal appeal, Weismantel immediately bought her a Coca-Cola and insisted, despite her visible reluctance, that she drink it. When she held the bottle in her hands, the old woman laughed in embarrassment, like a respectable matron caught trying on a miniskirt, and her granddaughter laughed too, incredulous at the sight. When the grandmother took a swig, the carbonation caught her by surprise, and she choked and snorted, spitting out the offending substance immediately and spending the next five minutes coughing and blowing her nose. She glared at her granddaughter as though she had tried to poison her, and made it very clear that this was the last soda that would ever cross her lips.

In Zumbagua, an older woman in bare feet, who speaks only Quichua, wears shawls and sashes, and whose body is marked by the decades of hard physical work, planting, weeding, and harvesting, hauling water and fuel, seems like someone who exists outside of the world economy. And indeed, she has never tasted Coca-Cola. Her young granddaughter, dressed in polyester and nylon, school educated and bilingual, who covets manufactured goods and foods of all kinds and plans to leave the parish to seek work in the city, does indeed present a stark contrast. But to say that in pockets of rural Ecuador

Coca-Cola is only now making inroads, albeit rapidly, is not to say
that sugar is an alien substance there. On the contrary: sugar is a
familiar friend in Zumbagua, even to the older generation. But the
sugars that grandmothers in the parish know and love do not come in
bottles, mixed with carbonated water; nor are they sparkling white
granules of highly processed cane sugar. The word mishqui (sweet
tasting) is far older than the introduction of cane sugar to the Andes
and so too is the experience of tasting sweetness.

Sweetness has been around a long time and human beings have
been interested in it for millennia. Sweet things, of which sugar cane
is only the most important source, have a long history in association
with the human species. Sugar cane diffused to the Asian mainland
from New Guinea millennia before the Christian Era, and reached the
New World with Columbus. Crystalline sugar is almost certainly
older than Christianity. Though it spread to many societies before
1492, its diffusion became almost explosive once large-scale production in the Americas had succeeded. Sugar cane's biggest competitor,
the sugar beet, did not become a commercially viable source until
well into the nineteenth century. Hence fine white granular sugar was
linked at first, and for centuries after, only to the juice of the cane;
not until around 1840 did a granular white beet sugar identical to cane
sugar become commercially practical.

Cane sugar, of course, is not the only food that tastes sweet.
Many fruits are dramatically sweet, as is honey. The sugars in fruits
include fructose, but not only fructose; the sweet taste of honey is
owing to fructose, dextrose, and other sugars. But the sugars in these
cases do have a taste readily linked to their sources. Honey enthusiasts, Claude Lévi-Strauss among them (1973:52), rhapsodize over the
distinctive tastes of different honeys, which are not pure in the same
way that granular sugar is pure. Anyone who has tasted the frankin-
cense-fragrant honey from the Hadhramaut, or who has a special
liking for confections in which maple sugar figures as an ingredient,
enjoys those tastes not only because they are sweet, but because they
are not only sweet. Beyond unalloyed, monolithic sweetness, then,
there are things that taste sweet and something else besides; they are
sweet and have a taste.

From this distinction we can easily derive another. It turns out that "pure" has more than one meaning. It can mean hygienic, germless, sanitary, "scientific," chemically simplified, etc. But pure can also mean natural, unadorned, and God-given (Mintz 1996:84-91). Such a distinction is useful to food technologists and advertisers, who sell us both meanings, alternatively or simultaneously. The "naturally pure" substance is rough-hewn, honest, unashamed, lacking in airs or artifice, homemade, straightforward, like maple syrup, honey, and certain mythological political figures. The chemically pure substance is refined, invariant, slick, modern, and (from the perspective of the other purists) lacking in personality, like white sugar and a whole different category of mythic politicians.

In the United States, not only sugar (sucrose) and honey taste sweet, but also, among many other things, high-fructose corn syrup, a maize-derived sugar now widely used in processed food. The important presence of HFCS in the American diet owes in part to former Cold War policies; only since a substantial hike in the domestic price of sugar, after the boycott of Cuban sugar, did it become commercially possible for high-fructose corn syrup to prosper in the U.S. market. Today, much more than half the processed sugars consumed in the United States are made from maize.

Of course, this list does not exhaust the sources of sweetness that figure in our foods. In almost all of these foods, however, sugar is used in a pure—that is to say, tasteless—form. Note that the sugars with tastes, such as maple sugar, honey, molasses, and turbinado sugar, are associated mainly with health foods, or with old-fashioned foods. People are prepared to be sanctimonious about them in a manner in which they are never sanctimonious about pure white sugar. Manufacturers capitalize upon the associations with health or tradition that such sugars invite by adding honey or maple flavoring to already sweetened processed foods such as breakfast cereals. In this case we can see the way in which pure sugar, a basic ingredient, is set apart from these flavorful sugars, which are then more likely to be categorized as savors or essences—more "genuine," "homey," "old fashioned," blah, blah—this side of their appeal often heightened with cinnamon, apples, currants, nuts, and raisins. The ideal marketing synthesis here is to counterbalance the doubled or tripled caloric count with a sufficiently comforting ambiance of wholesome-ness based on contrived imagery, so that the selling price can keep pace with the rising calories.

While such elaborate stratagems are required in the affluent and highly competitive North American market, the rural Latin American context affords simpler contrasts. In the Ecuadorian parish of Zumbagua, local people are far less conversant with the uses to which granular white sugar can be put. Yet even in the Andes, the differ-ence between white sugar and turbinado sugar expresses a contrast between the world of modernity and manufacturing and that of the old fashioned and the handcrafted. For if the old lady in the market disdained Coca-Cola as an unpleasant and unnecessary innovation, she would nonetheless be very unhappy if she had to run her kitchen without a supply of turbinado sugar, or *panela,* as it is called in the Spanish of the region. But this very dependence upon panela as a household staple marks her as a rural Indian. To most Ecuadorians, panela is an old-fashioned substance, prized because its strong flavor (not unlike that of maple sugar) immediately brings to mind images of grandmothers, of childhood, and of rural Ecuador. This heady mixture gets an adult repackaging in the *canelazo,* a sort of toddy made of boiling hot water and *trago* (cane alcohol) or rum with melted panela and cinnamon. (The name, which comes from *canela* [cinnamon], might be translated as a cinnamon blast or cinnamon punch.) Every mixologist has a secret recipe, but the results are always as drenched in nationalist sentiment as in sweetness.[2]

The town of Salcedo is in Cotopaxi Province, the same province of Ecuador where Zumbagua is located. But they are very different kinds of places. Salcedo is a white town, with many of the amenities of urban living (e.g., telephones, mail service, running water) still not available in Zumbagua. And rather than being perched up in the cold, windy, treeless zone known as the *páramo,* a place associated with llamas, condors, hailstorms, and Indians, Salcedo sits just south of the provincial capital of Latacunga and not far from the larger city of Ambato, in the middle of the wide, warm valley in the center of the Ecuadorian Andes. Every traveler knows it, for the town is bisected by the Pan American Highway. Its residents try to capture some of the traffic that roars past daily by offering a local specialty for sale, for which it is nationally known; a tasty mixture of panela sugar, cinnamon, and another ingredient having strongly sentimental associations with rural life. This latter is *máchica,* a finely ground toasted barley meal with a heady aroma, which is eaten either dry as a snack or immersed in hot water as a cereal similar to Cream of Wheat but with a distinctive taste and smell. All over Salcedo, but especially in houses and stores that front onto the Panamericana, windows sprout little handmade signs advertising canela. Drivers of taxis, trucks, and private cars make Salcedo a favorite stop, or at least a place about which to talk enthusiastically about stopping, and to reminisce nostalgically about the taste of panela and máchica as they drive past.

Of course, panela, like Coca-Cola, was once an exotic import to the Andes; yet this immigrant food (sugar), which traveled from Asia to the Middle East to Europe before arriving in the Americas, has come to signify everything that is most indigenous about Ecuadorian culture. This protean ability to reinvent itself as local and traditional in some circumstances, while in others appearing to be the very emblem of cosmopolitan modernity, has been part of sugar's appeal for a very long time. Today, not only Ecuadorian canelazos, but Dutch chocolate, American apple pie, and of course, British tea and crumpets, all use this tropical exotic to signify the familiarity of home. We can read in each case the residues of particular engagements of the local with the global as these took place at specific moments in history.

The diffusion of sugar to societies formerly without it occurred in a manner rather different from that of alcohol, tobacco, or the other proletarian hunger killers, coffee, tea, and chocolate; but it was in conjunction with these last three that the Europeans first became big sugar eaters. Together with tobacco and the three beverages, sugar was one of the first true commodities in the history of world capitalism. As such, its production and sale were integral to the success of a world economy that meshed different products, different forms of labor, different geographical regions, and different markets within a single whole. The case of heavily sweetened tea seems particularly dramatic; for the first time in world history two commodities drawn from opposite ends of the earth were transformed into a daily—often even thrice daily—dose for millions of working-class Europeans. The wholesale European acceptance of tea, coffee, and chocolate, together with sugar, as everyday necessities took a century or more to become fact. But once it happened, it never reversed itself. In recent papers, Bradburd and Jankowiak (1999) show how, during the expansion of capitalism, consumable goods such as sugar, coffee, and tobacco were then employed to persuade peoples on the margins of the world economy to participate in it.

But although the emergence of a world economy was a relatively slow and uneven process, it incorporated areas such as Zumbagua, which today seem so isolated and marginal that we might imagine that world history had, like Coca-Cola, only recently made its debut there. The tale of the old lady who spit out her Coke might appear, on the surface, to be one of an entirely localized, precapitalist economy of self-sufficient agriculturalists who are suddenly immersed in the world of money and exchange. But when we translate it into sugar—into the contrast between a bottle of Coca-Cola and a wheel of panela—it becomes apparent that the contrast is not between an absence of global history and its presence, but rather between successive modes of integration into the world economy.

In different eras, different regions emerged as key economic areas, to some extent rising and falling in importance in accord with external political and economic pressures. The Andes, which, when viewed from the perspective of late-twentieth-century North America, seem isolated and peripheral to the world economy, were once a major focus of investment and speculation for Spain. During the seventeenth and eighteenth centuries, Spain was a great world power, and her extractive interest in highland Latin America was intense. Rather than being isolated, the Andes of those centuries were subjected to intense colonialism, and the stark poverty, low agricultural productivity, and primitive farming technology to be found in Zumbagua today could as readily be interpreted as the result of centuries of brutally extractive economic systems as of mere isolation. Very few of the foods eaten in the parish are native to the Andes; most of them, however traditional or Indian they appear today, are themselves the residues of earlier economic, cultural, and biological invasions.

This history can be read in the complicated relationship between Quichua and Spanish in local language today. In Zumbagua, a sheep is called a llama, in recognition of the similarity in form and function between the European animal, introduced early in the seventeenth century, and its Andean counterpart. The llama itself is thus done out of a name; less important today than the sheep in the local economy, this native of the Andes is now referred to as a *runa* llama, an Indian sheep. These words are traces of a fundamentally important historical moment. It was with the introduction of the Spanish sheep (and the Incaic llama, which was possibly also introduced by the Spaniards) that the páramos of Zumbagua, which previously had probably been sparsely inhabited if at all, came into their own as a major productive zone. Far from having been an autochthonous society later subdued by the Spanish, Zumbagua in all probability first came into being as a result of the Spanish search for productive enterprises in regions of the Andes that did not yield the precious metals to be found in legendary Potosí.

The name of Zumbagua appears in 1600 in a list of places; it is described simply as a *hato de vacas,* a mere resting place for herders caring for cattle in the páramos; but it soon came to figure in documents as a property of worth. Documents relating to the sale of Zumbagua to the Augustinians, in whose hands the property was to remain for several centuries, are dated 1639. Nearby, other great estates in Apagua, Tigua, Mocata, Chugchilán, and elsewhere also took shape. A few "free" communities survived, but throughout the Sierra the residents of such free communities were drawn into the orbits of the haciendas as laborers, so that their position ultimately differed little from that of the hacienda Indians who lived as bound peons and whose own legal status was only minimally better than that of enslaved sugar plantation workers.

The expansion of the great landed estates, coupled with urban Spanish populations that were on the increase while the rural indigenous population was decimated by epidemics, created an acute labor crisis in the rural Sierra. The cities needed food, but the estates lacked the manpower to produce it. In response, Indians were relocated from elsewhere in the region (probably the warmer zones on the western slopes of the Andes) up to the cold páramos to herd sheep. A document of 1639 records a request to the Crown for permission to obtain more Indians to work as shepherds in Zumbagua; presumably such requests were successful, for by the end of the century Zumbagua had become a major wool producer. By 1780, it produced ninety thousand pounds of wool, all of which would have gone down to nearby towns such as Latacunga and Salcedo, where another group of Indian workers bent over looms in the *obrajes* (workshops) turning wool into cloth (Weismantel 1988:60-64; Carrera Colin 1981:155).

The Andean region was never a major producer of sugar for obvious reasons, but both to the west of Zumbagua in the warm coastal regions and to a lesser extent in the Amazonian tropics to the east, plantation agriculture was established and became increasingly important, gradually eclipsing highland hacienda production as the major engine of the economy.

Sugar came late to Ecuador; the first mills were built at the end of the nineteenth century. By 1909 there were only nine such enterprises, with a total annual production of 8,234 tons (Lentz 1992:23). Sometime in the first half of the twentieth century, the hacienda of Zumbagua built a sugar mill on the western slopes on land it owned some distance away. The children of white hacienda employees remember the arduous trips associated with managing these properties. Elderly ex-peons have more horrific memories. A man since passed away shared with Weismantel his vivid, nightmarish recollections of the month-long stint he, like other peons, was expected to put in at the mill in his youth. A fellow worker, unaccustomed to industrial machinery, was mangled by the mill press. Unable to save him, his companions held a wake over him through the night as he bled to death, and buried his body by a river that flowed down from the high country where he was born and which he would never again see.

Today, these small, primitive mills still exist; some are connected to stills and produce the fiery tragos for which the region is known. Others make panela (also called *rapadura*[3]) and send it up to the highland markets in big wheels wrapped in banana leaves. By the 1980s, it had become far more expensive than white sugar and was therefore disappearing from the diets of most Zumbagua households;

but for older people it was an absolute necessity, something on which they would spend money if they had it. Thus the difference between old fashioned and indigenous, and modern and more acculturated, was not between the absence and the presence of sugar but between which form of sugar was deemed necessary, and how much of a household's budget one was willing to spend upon it. Indeed, the liquid form of panela (called *miel,* honey) is a necessary ingredient in one of the most traditional of wedding dishes, in which squares of white cheese, salty and fresh-tasting, float in a bowl of this thick, brown, unutterably sweet substance.

The economic and historical meanings of panela and white sugar are found in how these products are produced and exchanged as well as in how they are consumed. In the early 1980s, Ecuador was an oil-producing OPEC nation suddenly rolling in cash. It used that prosperity to borrow still more and to engage in a spate of construction of highways and skyscrapers which created little long-term wealth and for which it would pay dearly in the 1990s, when oil prices plummeted and loan payments came due. But for a few short years, even men from a place as isolated and Indian as Zumbagua could find employment in the capital city doing construction work. And so the young men all went to Quito, and returned each weekend with money in their pockets and handfuls of candy for their children. The diet of the parish became more commodity based (and sugar dependent) than ever before, while the men learned to drink soft drinks rather than eat boiled potatoes during their lunch breaks on the job.

But not every man chose to go to Quito. An older pattern of wage labor had developed in the parish that took men down to the western slopes, away from the cities and the highlands, to cut sugar cane on the small, underfinanced little tropical plantations known as *fincas* that cling to the lower edges of the Andes. More men commuted to the city than chose to take up this kind of work, known locally as "machete work," because the wages were better in Quito. But those who liked the machete work had interesting things to say about it: like the coarse, strong-flavored brown sugar that was produced there, the labor relations on these fincas were something of an anachronism.

Men began going to the fincas for work in the early decades of the twentieth century, when the hacienda still claimed most residents' labor, as it would until the agrarian reforms of the 1960s. Although they arrived in the hot cloud forest zone as independent laborers, the relations were nonetheless paternalistic. Payment was partly in wages, partly in kind: workers received housing and meals, cane liquor to drink, and fruit, sugar cane, and other lowland products for their return to the highlands and their families. In the 1980s, older men, and some younger ones, were more comfortable with these terms than with the more impersonal structure of the construction site. They expected to be taken care of by their employers and to find in the meals cooked for them an indication of an affective bond as well as a work relationship.[4]

The same forces that brought the sugar cane to the New World brought enslaved Africans to Brazil, the Caribbean, and the southern United States, and entrepreneurial Catholic religious orders to regions such as Zumbagua. In such regions the consumption of substances and objects originating in distant lands increased only with glacial slowness, even though local labor and local products were important to the metropolitan center. The colonial regimes generally typical of Latin America did not link increasing productivity to increasing buying power or increasing consumption. In the late nineteenth century, differences between more and less traditional forms of extraction surfaced more clearly. Thus, for example, a contrast might be drawn between regions such as that surrounding Zumbagua, where traditional wool-producing haciendas held sway, and coastal plantation areas, such as that reported upon in Gillin's (1947) monograph on Moche.[5]

Even in these cases, however, the signs of a contrastive modernity are at best slight, if we look at consumption. Sugar plantations worldwide carry with them an ambience of modernity; but it lies mostly in their roads, machines, electricity, and water supply. The consumption of modernity in such settings involves relatively few products and takes on a rather meager, pinched form when it comes to concrete objects or substances for consumption. Yet it may not be experienced that way. Such pleasures as sweet drinks and sweet rolls can provide a sharp contrast to the everyday. In some contexts, carbonated beverages, pastries, and similarly exotic substances may afford symbolic identification of a kind with the foreign, the distant, and the powerful; at other times, as with the consumption of panela in Ecuador, this once-exotic food may instead be a part of the most homey and tradition-bound of eating rituals.

More often, however, sucrose, anciently emblematic of modernity, has been an early harbinger of a new era. As a key element in the diet of European proletarians, it was an invariable accompaniment to their moments of repose and renewed effort, as ubiquitous and desired as the stimulant beverages in which it was dissolved, or the tobacco with which it was so often consumed. It thereupon rediffused, or was produced, within that world the West had labeled "underdeveloped," recapitulating its functions for the peasants and rural proletarians of whom Weismantel (1988) has written.

CONCLUSIONS

This short chapter calls attention to three quite different issues. The first is directly connected to the intentions of the symposium for which it was originally written. The history of the diffusion of domesticated plants and animals is all sorts of history at once; economic, political, and cultural. The symposium and this volume call attention to some noteworthy cases. These are valuable because in spite of some ongoing and serious attempts, it seems likely that a complete world history of foods is still very far indeed from being written. We wanted to contribute to that history by adding, on the one hand, to what is known about a specific plant food source and, on the other, to our understanding of the changing usages that accompany the spread and modification of the foods created from such sources. By separating out to some extent the plant, the product, and the issue of taste, we hoped to better identify similarities and differences in the history of diffusion. This effort is consistent with an older anthropology's fascination with the material world and the many different ways in which people engage in innovation by putting their distinctive cultural stamp on the new and unfamiliar.

Second, the example of sugar in the Andes illuminates some aspects of the relationship between the local and the global. Those connections continue to puzzle, deceive, and mislead us; debates about which is "more important" or "decisive" in particular seem to us off the mark. By returning repeatedly to a dissection of the ways that the local may be predicated on the global, and at the same time to define locally what the global is, we return to the meanings of history in the making of the everyday. Ethnography without some consideration of agency strikes us as not fulfilling its most promising potentialities. At the same time, global generalities that ignore or wholly bypass the concretely ethnographic seem similarly to provide less illumination than they promise. Our aspiration is not to do both; rather, by doing them together, we hope to show that they are really one.

Finally, the stories of these three women and their sugar-eating habits tell us something about resistance precisely because of the impossibility of reading resistance, or its absence, into any of these examples. People are always learning new things, learning to use new objects, consuming new foods; e.g., cane sugar instead of fruit juices, brown sugar instead of white, soft drinks instead of sweetened barley. This happens with greater speed, more frequently, and in more places now than before; but it is not, after all, something happening for the first time. The diffusion of food sources, much of it at a very early point in world history, is an excellent case in point.

It is also true that people who are changing in these ways usually incorporate more than just the object or food into their daily lives. More often than not they develop new descriptive terms, contrive new times or rituals to mark usage, and otherwise redo the original practice. Trobriand cricket is not British cricket, and the parties at which Bolivian market women drink soft drinks are not really very much like the ones on Pepsi commercials after all.

But the appropriation, assimilation, incorporation or introjection of foreign materials and their reordering in culturally familiar terms is not of and in itself resistance. Velásquez and other successful market women love innovation as much as tradition; and although she has sometimes protested social injustice, Sofía has also taken advantage of poorer Bolivians when she had the chance. In either case, she has used new and old foods as she saw fit.

The case of the old lady who spat out her Coca-Cola is more ambiguous. Even an act such as this, which suggests some kind of intended resistance, is at most no more than that—an act intended as resistance. The propensity to attribute to all these processes such intentions, and to view such intentions as successful because they exist, is to make a serious analysis of resistance more difficult. Successful opposition to the forces that are unraveling indigenous cultural practices in Zumbagua would have to be far more organized and self-aware than this solitary, unthinking reaction, and the preference for older rather than newer forms of imports is not necessarily resistance at all.

We hope that the preceding ethnographic materials afford an accurate (if admittedly incomplete) picture of people changing in response to external forces of which they are not entirely aware, and with which they may be learning to deal, albeit, it seems to us, not very successfully. They are not successful because arrayed against them are impersonal market forces of great power with which they sometimes cannot avoid coping, but always asymmetrically. Their earnest efforts to "domesticate" those forces are no doubt resistant at times, and need to be documented—and celebrated—when they exist. But inference is not proof, intentions are not outcomes, and wishes alone do not make them so.

NOTES

1.   Mintz (1996:74-75) refers to a paper on the history of ice cream in Scotland, in which the Glasgow police are cited as giving testimony that ice cream was used there to bring young girls into prostitution.
2.   For a wonderful comparative study from Peru, see Orlove's (1982) "Tomar la Bandera: Politics and Punch in Southern Peru," in which a sweetened alcoholic drink has even more directly patriotic meanings.
3.   Called *raspadura* in the Dominican Republic, *rapadou* in Haiti, and by a wide variety of other locally specific names.
4.   There are two excellent studies of indigenous highland workers from a community in the province of Chimborazo who engage in temporary migration to work in a far larger and more modern sugar mill in coastal Ecuador (Lentz 1992, 1997).
5.   Gillin's (1947) study of Moche was made while residing in a hotel at some distance away because he was not able to find a place there, and he does not seem to have realized that he was really studying a rural proletarian sugar plantation community. Even Julian Steward, who wrote a few lines of

introduction, does not appear to have appreciated the special significance of Moche in the economic history of the Andean region.

THE CAPSICUMS IN OLD WORLD CULINARY STRUCTURES[1]

Susan Tax Freeman

This essay reviews the general characteristics of the New World genus Capsicum, *or peppers, and the circumstances of peppers' introduction, by Spaniards, into the Old World, where capsicums entered cuisines both as pungents and as vegetables. Attention is then focused upon the way in which hot and sweet peppers and the powdered condiment called paprika achieved signal importance and iconic status in two European cuisines, the Hungarian and the Spanish.*

A foodstuff might acquire a wide presence in the diets and cookery of different peoples, as is the case for the subject of this essay, peppers. But in a given place, its use in cookery (the mode in which it is presented in the essential units of the cuisine—dishes), the esteem in which it is held in relation to other foods, the associations it evokes, and the expressive and ideological bases for its esteem (high or low) can differ greatly. As anthropologists, we necessarily deal with foodstuffs in terms of cultural values along with their nutritional qualities. This brief essay is informed by a concept of cuisine as a cultural creation that possesses a structure; by a sense that food-stuffs—both well known and newly discovered—have or are given places in that structure (and sometimes evoke redefinition of parts of the structure); and by a vision of cookery as an art that must be seen as being as central to expressive culture as any of the other arts, even though it has received only marginal attention from most anthropologists. In a community of eaters, dishes must meet aesthetic standards, and most if not all dishes carry meaning. Historical changes in cuisines tell stories. These can be changes in the inventory of foodstuffs in use (such as the massive changes that ensued when the Old and New Worlds met), or changes in the composition of dishes, in styles of cooking and attitudes toward food(s), in culinary fashions.

The stories these changes tell are, of course, cultures' tales about themselves.

These informing concerns are large and invite much more extensive treatment than is possible or appropriate here, but they do guide looking at capsicums in their different kinds of entries into the Old World not only as domesticates and additions to the diet (as well as to commerce, which is not addressed here), but also as vehicles of expression about historical experience and group identity, even at a national level in the two cases presented here. I am much less pessimistic than Sidney Mintz (in this volume and elsewhere) about the persistence of "the ideologically normative function of consumption" and of true communities of eaters, perhaps even among urban professional Americans but certainly among those Europeans I know best! The issue of persistence, the large question of what constitutes a community of eaters even if they do not produce or cook their own food, and various other problems of modernity which Mintz suggests make an important agenda for future discussion.[2] But for now, in keeping with the focus of this symposium, I turn to consider a single foodstuff and some of its uses and meanings.

THE AMERICAN PEPPERS IN THE OLD WORLD

Plants of the genus *Capsicum* are native to South or Central America.[3] Their fruits today range from fleshy to thin-walled, large to small, sharply pungent to nonpungent and sweet, and from whitish to black, brown, red, yellow, orange, green, or purple in color while maturing. The majority of immature pods are green, however, and the majority of mature ones red, orange, or yellow. There are five domesticated species and several wild ones. The capsicums are deeply susceptible to modification by nature and the hand of man. Cross-fertilization can produce pungency in types that are usually sweet; selection and protection from this and other accidents of nature can produce more predictable varieties of fruit and do nowadays for commercial ends, which has long been the case in different places. Many if not all capsicum fruits can be used fresh and at different stages of maturity and many, including some of the fleshy ones, are dried and then used either whole or powdered. Both mature and immature fleshy peppers, whether sweet or pungent, are widely used as vegetables, raw or cooked; their less fleshy cousins are destined for condimentation of other foods. But pungency itself can be controlled to some degree by removal of seeds and veins before cooking or processing. The variety in each of the domesticated species, together with the alternative possibilities that govern the moment of their use and the nature of their use and processing, allow for an enormous range of flavors, textures, and culinary destinations in the hands of different cooks working in different cultural traditions.

Capsicums, or peppers, made a two-pronged entry into Old World culinary structures; one as a vegetable (although technically a fruit) and one as a condiment appreciated for its pungency or at least its intensity of flavor. Christopher Columbus was the first European to observe their use and remark on the qualities the hot peppers had in common with the black pepper (*Piper nigrum*) that came to Europe from India through the spice trade and which, of course, he was seeking. Columbus, in his journal, and shortly afterward Fernández de Oviedo (1535) and various other early observers immediately noted the position in the structure of the cuisines they knew into which the hot peppers (*ajís* or chilis) would fit: as a pungent condiment. Columbus wrote, "There is also much chili [ají], which is their pepper, of a kind more valuable than [black] pepper, and none of the people eat without it, for they find it very healthful."[4] And Fernández de Oviedo (1535; Libro VII, folio lxxv, a), who wrote about the ubiquity of peppers in native gardens and in the diet, says, "Axí is a plant of which the Indians make use and use in the place of pepper [*pimienta*]. . . . And it is no less agreeable to Christians and does no less for them than it does for the Indians" (my translation).

The early observers learned and accepted New World users' judgments that hot peppers offered, in addition to their culinary attraction, analgesic, stomachic, and digestive qualities. Today, of course, the active ingredient capsaicin has been studied and the beneficial qualities of chilis and peppers in general confirmed. In fact, a popular literature in the United States today is almost messianic on the subject of capsaicin, and hot peppers are enjoying a huge culinary vogue. (Among other things, this obscures the role and qualities of the less pungent peppers.) In one popular book, Naj (1993:xv), a journalist, claims that "the fruit . . . broadened the world's taste spectrum to include pungency alongside sweet, sour, bitter, and salty," as if there had been no pungency in the pre-Columbian Old World!

In fact, pungency (with varied chemical bases, physiological effects, and flavors) is ubiquitous. Europe alone had mustards, horseradish, onions, garlic, turnips and radishes, sharp cresses, and probably many other edible plants to add pungency to foods, and through trade came three esteemed sources—ginger, black pepper, and (from the west coast of Africa) melegueta pepper (*Aframomum melegueta*), a member of the cardamum family known as "Guinea pepper" and "grains of paradise," the focus of an active trade that gave the Guinea coast the name of "Grain Coast" in Europe. It was into this inventory that the hot capsicums were received. In such places as China, *fagara,* now called Szechuan pepper, and sharp cresses as well as ginger and other pungents, including true pepper, some of them traded for, occupied the niche that was to receive the hot capsicums, while India was, of course, the homeland of the true pepper plants whose name was extended to such unrelated pungents as Szechuan "pepper," Guinea "pepper," and capsicum "peppers."[5]

The second prong of the capsicums' entry into Old World use was as a vegetable; the intensely flavored but mostly nonpungent fleshy peppers. They extended the realm of vegetables in a host of cuisines from one end to the other of the Old World. Indeed, the large, fleshy vegetable peppers we know today as "sweet peppers" are undoubtedly the product of selective management which occurred in the Old World after the peppers' arrival there. Aboriginal forms were mostly smaller, and nonpungent peppers, as Long-Solís (1998) points out in the case of Mexico, did not and still do not have as much attraction as vegetable food for native eaters as they have in other parts of the world. Where sweet peppers are important as vegetables, they are eaten both raw and cooked and bring large amounts of vitamins A and C to the diet. Cooks in virtually all the Mediterranean countries, the Middle East, and the Balkans seized upon this vegetable which was, in the words of one Spanish writer, "the first-known vegetable that did not need to be hollowed out beforehand," and they stuffed it (Ríos and March 1992:15). So peppers joined the stuffed cabbage or eggplant and the New World zucchini and tomato as part of an entrée ensemble that usually also contained meat. Stuffed peppers are a dramatic example of a dish with many national homes across a continuous area of the Old World, but in other parts (as we well know) peppers are also found stir-fried, curried, stewed, fried in tempura batter, pickled, and in multitudes of salads and garnishes, raw and cooked.

The pungent capsicums have been called by various authors "the first democratic spice" (Weiss 1983:10) or "the universal and democratic spice" (Terrón 1992:303). Weiss, a Hungarian author, and Terrón, a Spanish one, refer, of course, to the ease with which even humble people can grow and preserve peppers and thereby condiment their food without recourse to the costly products of the spice trade. I will now turn in more detail to those two authors' nations to help underline the position that foodstuffs can assume in a national sense of self.

Hungary and Spain, as far as I know, are the only Old World nations in which capsicums and their products (principally ground paprika) are for themselves (as opposed to their use in such admixtures as curry) considered so essential to the cuisine that people cannot imagine (and often do not know) that their forebears ever did without them. Both nations claim to have invented paprika, of which both produce supreme but quite different types, using different varieties of *Capsicum annuum.*[6]

Columbus presented peppers at the Spanish Court in 1493 on return from his first voyage (Martyr de Angleria [or Anghiera] 1966:361); and their use and cultivation appear to have spread rapidly: by at least the middle of the sixteenth century, observers reported them in gardens everywhere. Although they were presented first at Court, they clearly spread rapidly down the social structure to become the "universal and democratic spice" that peppers (or *pimentón,* the Spanish word for paprika) now are (Terrón 1992). In Hungary, on the other hand, where peppers were probably introduced by Turks in Ottoman times as foodstuffs widely cultivated to provision Ottoman troops in their expanding orbit of control, peppers entered the social structure at the humble end and were, at first, slighted by the aristocracy. However, by the nineteenth century, capsicums had begun to define the most essential flavor of Hungarian dishes, which paprika entered in combination with lard and onions and often also, at a later stage in cookery, with sour cream (Gundel 1993; Kaneva-Johnson 1995; Lang 1971; and Szathmary 1992). It was Hungary's name for peppers and paprika that was exported worldwide in connection with the powdered pepper product.

Hungarian cooks used the capsicum expressively to distinguish themselves and their cuisine from the rest of Europe. In fact, Hungary is different from her neighbors: a land settled late by speakers of a non-Indo-European language, straddling East and West, first emerging from Europe's margins and under the thumb of Ottoman Islam, and then forming part of a powerful European empire (the Hapsburg) from whence Hungary could show off to Europe a distinctive cuisine, ultimately unified from bottom to top of the social structure in a collective use of paprika. Spain, too, sat at Europe's margins, for centuries touched by Islam, to emerge after 1492 at the helm of her own great empire, and with a newly distinctive cuisine that became part of the collective sense of self and self-presentation to others.

The year 1492 saw the final separation of Spain from Islam and the discovery of the New World, capsicums included, along with maize, tomatoes, chocolate, pineapples, tobacco, sweet potatoes, beans, squashes, eventually potatoes, and other cultivars on which Spain first held a monopoly, not only of access and provision but also of knowledge. The first generation of Spaniards in the New World used and tasted these items in contact with the living populations who used them regularly, thus learning on the spot that they were comestible and not poisonous. In this way, Spanish cuisine represented in Europe an avant garde at the same time that Spain expelled from her soil the non-Christian contact of the Middle Ages, doing a symbolic service for much of the rest of Europe. These events are encapsulated in two recipes.

Pimientos rellenos, stuffed peppers, are a national dish to Spaniards. To chop meat finely and stuff vegetables with it was in medieval Spain a hallmark of Muslim or Jewish cooking and, since 1492, is mostly to be found in North Africa and the Middle East; lands of Hispano-Moorish and Sephardic refuge after the expulsion from Spain.[7] The principal remaining dish was meatballs, whose very name, *albóndigas,* is derived from Arabic. Spanish cooks first christianized the meatball by putting the traditional cured fatback (*tocino*), and/or ham or fresh pork into the meat mixture. Then the baptized albóndiga was buried inside a roasted sweet pepper (or shall we say dressed up in it?) for presentation to the world; it was sometimes even rebaptized with tomato sauce. This dish is sometimes found depicted on picture postcards.

A second recipe, that for *chorizo* sausage, has been made in Spain since before the advent of peppers but was earlier flavored with black pepper, ginger, and a bit of vinegar. (Hungarians had similarly used ginger for pungency in sausages.) Today, the dictionary definition of *chorizo* carries with it the inclusion of pimentón in the *adobo,* or spice mixture with which the meat is seasoned. Use of the word chorizo in Spain today eclipses use of *longaniza,* a word which is probably much older than peppers in Spain, has more European connections than chorizo, but is less closely associated with paprika (Covarrubias 1989:771-72; and Mathiesen 1993). Paprika and garlic adobo is widely used, especially for pork, and seasoned pork or chorizos themselves enter such a variety of dishes, from paella to legume stews and meat sautés, that the repertoire of Spanish cuisine is not achievable today without capsicums. The sweet red peppers used for paprika can also enter sausages on their own, before grinding, and are known simply as *pimientos choriceros* (sausage peppers). The chorizo itself defies translation: when a French or other European recipe calls for it in a "Spanish-style" dish, the cook is simply instructed to procure chorizo, which is central to the Spanish larder and enters the Larousse lexicon on its own.

Chorizo is untranslatably Spanish as paprika and *gulyas* are untranslatably Hungarian. They represent their respective cuisines in the wider world and at home. No Spaniard or Hungarian can legitimately claim, as they sometimes do, that peppers "have been here forever." But precisely because of the capsicums' variety and manipulability and their selective management in Spain and Hungary for Spanish and Hungarian culinary ends, each nation can legitimately claim to have invented paprika and each can truly assert that the pepper is, like the national dishes into which it enters, uniquely its own.

NOTES

1. This essay is dedicated to the memory of Louis Szathmary in thanks for his generous friendship and aid to my work in culinary history in his last years. I thank his estate for providing the copy herein cited of his unpublished paper on paprika.

2. Mintz (1996) opens many of these subjects to inquiry in his *Tasting Food, Tasting Freedom*. While he doubts that we can address cuisines on a national level, I do just that here, albeit with caution and in the interest of opening discussion on that subject.

3. In addition to standard encyclopedic and botanical sources, see such sources as Andrews (1984), DeWitt and Bosland (1996), and Long-Solís (1998), among many others.

4. This was written in the journal of the first voyage of 1492-1493 (Dunn and Kelley 1988:340-41).

5. In addition to standard encyclopedic and botanical sources, see such sources on the spread, early uses, and management of food plants (and other foodstuffs) as Root (1980) and Ward (1929). On China see Simoons (1991); on India see Achaya (1994); for a recent review of African materials see Hall's (1991) essay and the references in Viola and Margolis (1991:266).

6. On the different varieties of *Capsicum annuum* used in Spanish and Hungarian paprikas see DeWitt and Bosland (1996). On the invention of paprika, for Spain see Terrón (1992:303 and elsewhere); for Hungary see Lang (1971:130). The claim is made tenuous for Hungary because of the Turkish source of the cultivar and the heavy Turkish use of peppers, whether or not they were ground into paprika. The Spanish language distinguishes more clearly the fruits from the powder made from them and makes their separate uses more discernible for the historian. References to powdered peppers are at least as early as 1611 (see Covarrubias's (1989 [1611]) dictionary under *pimiento*). But Spain's claim is made tenuous because it is difficult to ignore that the New World techniques of drying and/or toasting peppers before grinding them for addition to sauces produce a kind of paprika, too. That primitive paprika manufacture may have occurred in dozens of places does not diminish the fact of paprika's elevation to an industry and a culinary icon in both Hungary and Spain and differentiates each from its original sources of capsicums. For Hungary contrast Gundel (1993) or Weiss (1983), among many others, with contemporary Turkish usage as recorded in Algar (1985), for one example. For Spain, contrast widely recorded Mexican cookery techniques with, for one

example, those of Barrera (1996), a chef working in Extremadura near one center of Spain's paprika production.

7.   For a more extensive study of the meaning condensed in this dish, see my separate study of stuffed peppers (Freeman 1999).

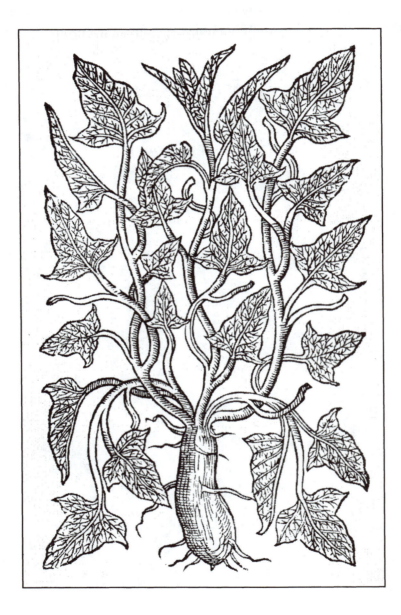

THE PERILOUS POTATO AND THE TERRIFYING TOMATO[1]

Stanley Brandes

Despite the long-term impact of the Andean potato and Meso-american tomato on European agriculture and cuisine, neither of these New World plants received immediate acceptance in Europe. This essay explains why. Relying primarily on linguistic evidence, the chapter demonstrates that these foods were originally associated with the fruit of the Garden of Eden. Hence they were both feared as poison and coveted as aphrodisiacs. The essay also explores medical, psychological, and related factors which influenced feelings toward the potato and tomato in early modern Europe.

History shows that edible plants diffuse from one locale to another in a highly unpredictable fashion. Potatoes originated in the Andes, and yet they spread most widely by ship, not land, thereby reaching Mexico not directly, but via Spain, more than a century after Europeans had become familiar with them. The potato probably first arrived first on North American shores no earlier than 1719, brought from Ireland by immigrants who settled in Londonderry, New Hampshire (Ensminger et al. 1994:1815). The wild progenitor of the tomato (a kind of cherry tomato, *Lycopersicum cerasiforme*) was probably native to Ecuador and Peru. Yet the actual cultivation of tomatoes began in Mesoamerica, and got to the Andes only after Spaniards introduced the crop in the eighteenth century (Ensminger et al. 1994:2110).

It is well known that food from one part of the world does not automatically appeal to people from another. Even under optimal conditions, foods generally take generations to become accepted. Kiwis have long been part of the Pacific diet and yet they did not become generally available in European and American markets until the 1980s. Only since the 1980s, too, has olive oil become a widely acceptable vegetable shortening in American cooking, centuries after northern Europeans and their descendants learned about Mediterranean cuisine.

If such resistance characterizes the modern world, just imagine past times, when means of communication, agricultural knowledge, buying power, and the appreciation of innovation were not nearly what they are today. The initial encounter between Europe and the Americas in the fifteenth and sixteenth centuries indisputably resulted in the incorporation of countless American foods into the European diet. Potatoes, tomatoes, chocolate, vanilla, squash, lima beans, French beans, peanuts, red and green peppers, among numerous other plants, managed eventually to achieve popular acceptance. But with few exceptions they did so slowly, only after lengthy periods through which agricultural experimentation, culinary trial, and aesthetic appeal eventually overcame their initially dubious reputations. And the reluctance to engage exotic domesticates is not over; witness the persistent European resistance to pumpkin. Of all the American squashes, this remains a holdout, a living testimony to the observation that culinary preferences die hard.

Few would dispute the ubiquitous and profound long-term effects of at least three major New World crops: potatoes, tomatoes, and maize. However, none of these plants, with their countless culinary and nutritional virtues, received rapid European acceptance. The historical resistance to maize consumption in Western Europe, which endures in many areas today, originally rested primarily, if not exclusively, on the perceived connection between maize, illness, and social suffering, as well as on the negative ethnic and religious connotations (Moorish and Islamic) with which maize came to be associated (Brandes 1992). Potatoes and tomatoes suffered from some of the same prejudices, yet followed a somewhat different trajectory from maize; Europeans accepted these plants as comestibles slowly, but eventually embraced them wholeheartedly. As with maize, the initial reputation of these food crops upon reaching Europe in large part determined the pace of their penetration into Europe. Unlike maize, however, potatoes and tomatoes were not sullied by negative ethnic associations. It was above all their reputed sexual and medicinal properties that influenced the attitude of Europeans toward these plants. Their partly justifiable reputation for being poisonous remained an issue well into the nineteenth century.

Of these two plants, potatoes have probably received the greater historical attention. The potato (*Solanum tuberosum*) is a member of the nightshade family (*Solanaceae*), which also includes the tomato, capsicum peppers, tobacco, and eggplant, but is unrelated to yams and sweet potatoes (Ensminger et al. 1994:1814). The potato was first cultivated between 4,000 and 7,000 years ago in the Andes mountains of what is now Bolivia and Peru and was the staple of the area (Ensminger et al. 1994:1815). Like other American crops, the potato entered Europe via Spain, whose Iberian-bound ships were stocked with potatoes. Potato consumption during long oceanic voyages helped prevent the onset of scurvy. Although seafarers were well aware of this valuable property (Ensminger et al. 1994:1815), and even though they were championed by agronomists and other scientists of the day, potatoes initially had a bad reputation and did not become widely accepted until the nineteenth century.

One impediment was the potato's strange appearance. Redcliffe Salaman, who knew more about the social history of the potato than anyone in his time or since, reminds us that this food was "the first edible plant in Europe to be grown from tubers and not from seed. . . . [Until] then no similar plant . . . was grown which bore on underground stems numerous white or flesh-coloured nodules" (Salaman 1949:112). Salaman presents evidence that "[t]he white nodular tubers, with bulbous finger-like growths, may well have recalled the deformed hands and feet of the unfortunate leper, the dreaded outcast of the Middle Ages and the Renaissance" (Salaman 1949:112). In 1619 potatoes were banned from Burgundy because they were thought to produce leprosy (Salaman 1949:112). This belief endured well into the eighteenth century. As late as 1748, the parliament of Besançon forbade the growing of potatoes as a way to stop the disease from spreading (Toussaint-Samat 1992:717). Potatoes also were deemed responsible for other maladies, among them alcoholism. Nietzsche, for example, stated that "[a] diet that consists predominantly of rice leads to the use of opium, just as a diet which consists predominantly of potatoes leads to the use of liquor" (quoted in Root 1980:378).

The reputation of potatoes for being poisonous was in part a consequence of religious beliefs. Since potatoes are not mentioned in the Bible, eating this food was initially, in the words of Salaman (1949:116), "akin to eating the forbidden fruit of Eden, a sinful act which, even if its effects were physically harmless, was bound to create a feeling of personal guilt, which demanded some kind of expiation lest the individual be smitten with some dreaded disease." Regardless of whether this religious motivation for avoiding potatoes was widespread, there is no doubt that Europeans initially perceived potatoes as a health risk.

It was common, in fact, for Europeans to attribute positive or negative medicinal properties to American crops in general. Potatoes were suspect from the outset, since they belong botanically to the poisonous nightshade family. Food analyst Waverly Root (1980:386) speculates that immediately after the Conquest potatoes actually might have been occasionally poisonous, sometimes causing the skin to break out in a rash. In fact, as Johns (1996:69-70) points out, potato tubers contain chemicals that act as defenses against attack by herbivores and pathological micro-organisms. "The cohort of chemical defenses in potatoes act in concert to protect the plants from herbivores and pathogens; conversely, they present complex detoxication problems for animals exploiting potatoes" (Johns 1996:70), which is to say that they are potentially toxic. Wild potatoes have an unusually high degree of toxicity, due to their glyco-alkaloid content. Potato poisoning, with severe gastrointestinal disturbance and vomiting as the main symptoms, result from eating these and other unprocessed potatoes (Johns 1996:70).

Root (1980:386) observes that "[s]ome housewives still, when they cut open a potato and find it lightly tinged with green, throw it away instead of cooking it. The green color betrays the presence of solanine, which is indeed a poison, common to plants of the potato's family, the Solanaceae. . . . Our modern potatoes do not contain a large enough proportion of solanine to bother anybody; but the potatoes of the sixteenth century contained higher dosages of it. Even Renaissance potatoes were not capable of killing anybody, but they did sometimes cause the skin to break out in a rash," an eventuality that of course confirmed the suspicion that potatoes produced leprosy.

Although potatoes were initially believed to be poisonous, they were also perceived as restorative; particularly sexually. It was perhaps for this reason that the Western European elite were the first to embrace potato consumption enthusiastically. Salaman (1949:106) found in a medical treatise published in 1620 that one Dr. Tobias Venner advised eating the potato "to incite to venus." The same year, playwright John Fletcher had one of his characters declare, "I have fine potatoes, Ripe potatoes! Will your Lordship please to taste a fine potato? 'Twill advance your wither'd state. Fill your Honour full of noble itches." About a century later, William Salmon's Herbal declared that potatoes prevented "fluxes of the bowels," had lots of nutrients, and cured consumption. "Being boiled, baked or roasted," he continued, potatoes "are eaten with good butter, salt, juice of oranges or lemons, and double refined sugar. . . . They increase seed and provoke lust, causing fruitfulness in both sexes" (quoted in Salaman 1949:106). Andean Indians perhaps held the same belief, given that the Aymara word *choque* means both potato and testicle. South American conquistadors first called the potato *turma de tierra,* or earth testicle. Even today, in the authoritative Spanish language dictionary of the Real Academia Española, potato is listed as one of the common meanings of *criadilla,* yet another Castilian term for testicle.

The potato's reputation as an aphrodisiac grew throughout the eighteenth century, during which it became popular among workers and peasants. In Ireland, of course, it became the staple food of the poor. Traveler David Henry, writing in 1771, used the Irish case to demonstrate the potato's potent properties. Writes Henry (1771:275), the potato "is favorable to population; for it has been observed, that in the western parts of Ireland where it is almost the only diet of the labouring poor, it is no unusual thing to see six, seven, eight, ten and sometimes more children, the issue of one couple, staring almost naked out of a miserable cabin. . . ." The potato, Henry (1771:275) declares, "creates a vigorous population." And of course it was during the time that the potato became widely accepted throughout Europe that enormous population growth occurred. Historians and demographers have long debated whether the vastly increased consumption of potatoes during the eighteenth century actually stimulated population growth or was an agricultural and culinary response to that growth (e.g., Boserup 1966; van Bath 1966).

What is certain is that in northern Europe, where potatoes first took popular hold, "just one acre planted to potatoes could feed a family of five or six, plus a cow or pig, for most of a year. The plant could grow in a wide variety of soils and it required no tools other than a spade and hoe; it matured within three or four months, as compared to the well over half a year for grain crops, and it had the advantage of a high nutritional value" (Farb and Armelagos 1980:76). For this reason, potatoes in Italy, Spain, and elsewhere became food for the poor (Root 1980:381). Diderot, writing in the eighteenth century, provides evidence of the potato's popularity among the poor and corresponding disdain with which it was regarded by the rich: "This root, no matter how you prepare it, is tasteless and floury. It cannot pass for an agreeable food; but it supplies a food sufficiently abundant and sufficiently healthy for men who ask only to sustain themselves. The potato is criticized with reason for being windy, but what matters windiness for the vigorous organisms of peasants and laborers?" (quoted in Root 1980:378).

European wars from the sixteenth century on were among the important factors stimulating potato production. Grains of all types were generally stored, thereby providing potential booty for plundering armies of hungry soldiers, while potatoes could be left in the ground until they were ready to be consumed. This quality, together with the ecological suitability of potato production to the requirements of a burgeoning European population, eventually erased prejudices against this crop (Toussaint-Samat 1992:717-25).

While the potato has enjoyed rich and abundant scholarly attention, other successful American crops have not. Given its enormous influence on European cuisine, the tomato has suffered most in this regard. The problem is not lack of historical interest. It is rather the highly perishable quality of the plant itself, which strictly reduced its transportability and kept it for centuries within the confines of kitchen gardens, thereby assuring that it would receive only minimal documentary recording. It appears neither in censuses, nor marketing reports, nor tax registers until relatively late in history. Nonetheless, Smith's (1994) recent treatment of the topic does much to synthesize what is known of the tomato in past times and to present a balanced, scholarly presentation of knowledge that was heretofore based on hearsay.

Botanically, the tomato (*Lycopersicon esculentum*) is a fruit, specifically a berry, notable as other berries are for its firm skin, hard seeds, and cavities filled with a jelly or mucous-like substance (Macrae et al. 1993:4580). Despite the fact that the tomato is a fruit and the potato a tuber, the two plants passed through many of the same stages on their road to European popularity. The coincidence in part derives from the fact that the tomato, like the potato, bears resemblance to plants of the poisonous nightshade family. Europeans were already familiar with the adverse effects of these plants through the indigenous presence of belladonna and mandrake. Hence it is not surprising that the tomato early on earned a reputation for toxicity.

Italian naturalist Pierandrea Mattioli was the first European to write about the tomato. In 1544, he described it as a sort of eggplant and dubbed it *mala aurea* (golden apple), which in subsequent editions of his herbal he changed to *mala insana* (unhealthy apple) (Root 1980:511). In fact, as Root (1980:512) reminds us, the leaves and stems of both potatoes and tomatoes are poisonous and have been known to kill cattle grazing off limits. If the first Europeans to try potatoes and tomatoes accidentally ate these parts of the plant, rather than the potato root or the tomato fruit, they might very well have suffered from food poisoning.

Italians have always been the most ardent culinary champions of the tomato, so it is not surprising that they were the first to adopt this food on a large scale (Root 1980:512). In its original Mexican form, the tomato plant "produced round marble-sized fruits, resembling the cherry tomato we know today" (Toussaint-Samat 1992:707). The people of southern Spain first used tomatoes, mixed with chiles, as the basis for a spicy sauce. They diffused quickly to what is now Italy through the Kingdom of Naples (Toussaint-Samat 1992:707), which had come under Spanish rule in 1522, only a few years after the introduction of these new items to Spain itself. Initially, in Italy as elsewhere, preventative measures were taken to avoid the presumed toxic effects of the plant. Two preparatory techniques were applied: first, to cook the fruit for literally hours, and second, to mix it with vinegar and spices. Perhaps these methods were designed to neutralize the humoral quality of coldness (for a thorough discussion of hot-cold classifications as scientific medicine, see Foster 1994), which was applied to the tomato. Herbalist John Gerard writes of tomatoes in 1597,

The whole plant is of a ranke and stinking savour. . . . The Golden Apple with the whole herbe it selfe is cold, yet not so fully cold as Mandrake. . . . But in my judgment it is very cold, yea perhaps in the highest degree of coldnesse: my reason is because I have in the hottest time of summer cut away the superfluous branches from the mother root, and cast them carelessly in the allies of my Garden, the which (notwithstanding the extreme heate of the Sun, the hardness of the trodden allies, and at that time when no rain at all did fal) have growne as fresh as where I cast them as before I did cut them off: which argueth the great coldnesse contained therein. (Quoted in Root 1980:511)

In Renaissance Europe, it was essential to gauge the humoral properties of previously unknown plants so as to measure their effect on the body, and hence health.

As late as the nineteenth century, health warnings were issued against the tomato in England and the United States, because it was said to cause cancer (Root 1980:514). English herbalist William Salmon, writing in 1710, records the existence of tomatoes in the Carolinas, which is the first evidence of tomatoes in present United States territory. One popular legend has it that in 1840, "a daredevil named Colonel Robert Gibbon Johnson, standing on the steps of the courthouse of Salem, New Jersey, defied death publicly by eating a raw tomato" (Root 1980:512). Smith (1994:3-10) has compiled dozens of examples of this legend, most placing the event in 1820. Since 1987, he says, the people of Salem have held an annual Robert Gibbon Johnson Day in which a re-enactment of the tomato-eating legend is performed on the courthouse steps (Smith 1994:5).

Despite initial misgivings about the safety of eating tomatoes, Europeans as early as the seventeenth century adopted the plant widely as an ornamental. In the words of seventeenth-century French agronomist Olivier de Serres (quoted in Root 1980:513), tomatoes are "marvelous and golden," and "serve commonly to cover outhouses and arbors." The 1760 edition of the Vilmorin seed catalog listed tomatoes with ornamental plants, although by 1778 they were also categorized as a type of food (Root 1980:513). Testimony from

Brillat-Savarian (1803; quoted in Toussaint-Samat 1992:707) indicates that in the early nineteenth century tomatoes had been known in Paris for only a few years:

> This vegetable or fruit, as one may call it, was almost wholly unknown in Paris 15 years ago. We owe its introduction to the great influx of those southerners brought by the Revolution to the capital, where most of them made their fortunes. Very expensive at first, it then became very common, and might be seen in great baskets-full in La Halle last year, while before it used to be sold by the half-dozen . . . be that as it may, tomatoes are a great blessing to good cookery. They make excellent sauces which go well with every kind of meat.

According to testimony from 1752, the English first employed tomatoes in soups and sauces, mixed with pepper, vinegar, salt, and other spices, presumably as a way of warding off the toxic effects of the plant (Root 1980:514).

As with potatoes, tomatoes long held a reputation as an aphrodisiac. Perhaps it was the tomato's physical resemblance to the mandrake (also of the nightshade family) that ultimately bears responsibility for this reputation. The mandrake appears in the Book of Genesis, where Rachel and Leah employ its roots as a love potion. The word for mandrake in Hebrew, *dudaïm,* actually translates as love apples or love plants (Smith 1994:12). In fact, eggplants, which originated in Southeast Asia and also belong to the nightshade family, were also called love apples for a time after their introduction into Europe. In all three cases (mandrake, eggplant, and tomato), leaf structures, flowers, and fruits are similar. Swiss naturalist Konrad Gesner painted a watercolor in 1553 of a small, red-fruited plant, to which he gave the Latin name *poma amoris* (love apple). Smith (1994:13) speculates reasonably that it was the tomato's resemblance to the fruit of the mandrake that induced Gesner to give it this name. Or it might have been Gesner's familiarity with the work of Luca Ghini, a sixteenth-century Italian botanist who founded Europe's first botanical garden at Pisa. Ghini called the tomato *amatula,* a Latin word that denotes possession of an aphrodisiac quality (Smith 1994:13). Eighteenth-century writer Edward Long claimed of tomatoes that "Spaniards esteem them aphrodisiacs" (quoted in Smith 1994:20), and in the early nineteenth century Dr. John Cook Bennett, a great promoter of the tomato's supposed medicinal properties, claimed that it had a "reputation of being stimulant, or aphrodisiacal," which he learned from the British *Cyclopedia or Universal Dictionary* (Smith 1994:105). Whether or not the tomato retained its reputation as a sexual stimulant, the term was still being used throughout the English-speaking world even into the twentieth century.

Potatoes and tomatoes, therefore, shared ambivalent receptions into Europe. They were both feared as poisonous, and yet coveted for their presumed potent sexual properties. It is hard to believe that these seemingly contradictory reputations were the coincidental product of random fantasies. The explanation for their simultaneous presence is by no means certain. Nonetheless, we may speculate that there was some religious foundation for European reactions to American plants and animals. Both potatoes and tomatoes resembled strange types of apples: in the case of potatoes, *pommes de terres* (earth apples); in the case of tomatoes, golden apples or love apples. Was not the fruit of the Garden of Eden (traditionally an apple) also simultaneously dangerous and sexually charged? Could it be that these unfamiliar New World substances, bearing no actual biblical reference, initially assumed the symbolic meaning of their mythological equivalent in the Book of Genesis? Whatever future research along these lines might determine, there is no doubt that potatoes and tomatoes, from the eighteenth century on, definitively and profoundly transformed European cuisine. Slow to be accepted, arousing a mixture of curiosity, admiration, and suspicion, they eventually demonstrated their culinary and nutritional virtues to win a permanent and prominent place on the table.

Finally, why did the potato and tomato achieve earlier and more widespread success in Western Europe than maize? As elaborated in an earlier article (Brandes 1992), the earliest names used for maize imply not only a Turkish, but also a Moroccan, Moorish, and generally Arabic origin for that plant. These particular labels should remind us that the year 1492 marked the Spanish discovery of America as well as the reconquest of Granada, which was the final death blow to nearly eight centuries of Islamic presence in the Iberian Peninsula. Ferdinand and Isabella, known as the Catholic monarchs, supported exploration as a means to power, wealth, and religious expansion. But they had no tolerance for faiths like Islam or Judaism which had thrived in their dominions and might compete with Roman Catholicism. Their successors, Charles V and Philip II, were equally fanatic in asserting the exclusivity of Roman Catholicism, expelling or murdering recidivist converts and setting up tribunals to ensure the religious purity both of their home subjects and applicants for immigration to America. The religious and political posture of these monarchs was so strident and effective that virtually all Spaniards came to consider Moors and Jews pariahs.

At the same time, wheat, for millennia the staff of life in the Mediterranean basin, was imbued with sacred significance—the same sacred significance it no doubt enjoyed both prior to and long after the fifteenth and sixteenth centuries. Consider the centrality of the wheat wafer at Mass, the priest's blessing over it, its transubstantiation into the body of Christ, its ritual consumption by the faithful, and its magical power to cleanse from sins. As late as the 1970s, throughout rural Spain one could still observe peasants marking a cross on a fresh loaf before cutting into it.

Under such political and religious circumstances, it is no wonder that most Spaniards and, indeed, Christians of the era rejected maize. For one thing, it is a grain, thereby placing it in conceptual competition with wheat. Of course, in the minds of most North Americans, maize and wheat are not substitutable items. Corn on the cob to us it simply a vegetable accompaniment to a meal, not the basis of it, and we think nothing of alternating between bites of bread and bites of corn. But we know from the sixteenth century herbals that corn was instantly defined as a subsistence grain, something that the more successful potatoes and tomatoes were decidedly not. When measured alongside wheat, which Europeans had relied on for centuries and which had come to assume such high symbolic and religious value, corn could not compete. This defeat was all the more certain given the erroneous linguistic association of maize with despised Islamic peoples. Spaniards of the era went to all lengths, including changes of name, fashion, occupation, and residence, to avoid being labeled an infidel. It is likely, in such an atmosphere of religious intolerance, that dietary patterns including consumption of pork and avoidance of corn played a role in defining and asserting ethnic and religious identity. In time, the avoidance of maize must have become so ingrained that it affected people emotionally to the point where it assumed the status of a true taboo.

As we have seen, symbolic religious associations, specifically to Genesis and the story of the Fall, initially contributed to the ambivalent attitude toward potatoes and tomatoes and their slow acceptance into the European diet. In the case of corn, however, religious meanings became inextricably linked to ethnic identity and national rivalries. Ethnic prejudice, never an important factor in the way potatoes and tomatoes were regarded, probably caused a tenacious resistance to maize consumption which lasts in many areas today.

NOTE

1. I thank Ellen Greenblatt for comments leading to stylistic improvement on an earlier version of this essay.

KUKU—"GOD OF THE MOTUITES": EUROPEAN TOBACCO IN COLONIAL NEW GUINEA[1]

Terence E. Hays

When European colonists arrived in Papua New Guinea, tobacco and the custom of smoking already were widespread but not universal. The newcomers quickly filled this void by introducing trade tobacco, which nearly everywhere was rapidly adopted. A "passion" for smoking was especially evident among those to whom tobacco was previously unknown or very new. The chemical properties of nicotine combined with an absence of cultural rules regarding its use to create a new "god."

Throughout Papua New Guinea there are myths that describe the local origins of tobacco and the custom of smoking. Despite such oral traditions (and more from Irian Jaya), virtually all modern scholars agree that tobacco in New Guinea is the American species, *Nicotiana tabacum,* and that its initial entry was almost certainly in northwestern Irian Jaya, not long after the Dutch introduced the plant to Java in 1601 and Ternate in 1605 (Haddon 1946; Riesenfeld 1951; Marshall 1981; Kocher-Schmid 1994). Over the next three centuries there were probably additional introductions by so-called Malay traders and plume-hunters along the northern coast, but the geographical distribution of the cultivation and smoking of tobacco in New Guinea when the significant presence of Europeans began in the nineteenth century is largely the result of a long process of gradual south- and southeastward diffusion.

During the period from the 1870s to the 1930s, when colonial administrators and others first contacted most of the indigenous groups of Papua New Guinea, knowledge of tobacco was said to be absent, or only recently acquired, among numerous peoples, almost all of whom lived in a broad swath covering the southeastern portions of this huge island (Hays 1991a). Thus the arrival of Europeans occurred as tobacco and smoking were perhaps inexorably making their way toward the ubiquity with which they are found today.

One must say "perhaps inexorably" because of course we cannot know whether or not the diffusion of tobacco and the custom of smoking would have continued along traditional trade routes as it had done for three centuries. In part, this is because the introduction of European goods disrupted many of these old trading networks (see, e.g., Hughes 1978). More importantly, Europeans themselves immediately began taking an active role in the process with the deliberate introduction of twist, or trade, tobacco, largely an American commercial product consisting of cured tobacco twisted into sticks and often soaked in rum or molasses. This product, which was followed later by commercial pipe tobacco in some areas and cigarettes almost everywhere, is the main concern of this chapter.

The colonial literature of New Guinea is replete with comments by administrators, explorers, missionaries, and traders on the degree to which twist tobacco quickly became a kind of currency, almost universally convertible along the coasts into copra, food, labor, land—whatever one wanted. Representative of this view is the report of Theodore Bevan (1890:3), an early explorer on the south coast of British New Guinea:

[I]n the autumn of 1884 I made up my mind to visit New Guinea.
It was described as a land of gold, yet where a fig of tobacco would buy more than a nugget of the precious metal had power to purchase. . . .

Indeed, one could buy a lot, even gold, with little investment. While conversion rates varied regionally, and over time as inflation began in some areas, Europeans in the period from the 1870s to the 1930s typically paid about a penny or less for a stick of tobacco which yielded coconuts for the burgeoning copra trade, food, labor, gold, and converts (or at least church-goers) for the missions. For example, in the early colonial period an economic mainstay for many Europeans was the copra industry, which demanded large numbers of coconuts. These were readily supplied by local people even when, at Tauwara, in Milne Bay, in 1891, the price received by local people for their copra was, in the view of the administrator, Sir William MacGregor (1892:32), "far from encouraging; they get two-fifths of a pound of trade tobacco for a full sack of copra. If they sell the cocoanuts, they get for twenty-eight cocoanuts the twenty-fifth part of a pound of tobacco. It is wonderful that they care to take so much trouble for such poor returns." Coconuts were also of interest for their food value, as with the gold miners on Misima Island in the late 1890s, who paid "only one stick of tobacco for forty nuts" (Nelson 1976:40).

In addition to food, all European colonials (as keen on other forms of work as they were on gardening) required labor, and this too was available in return for tobacco. On Goodenough Island, "two sticks of tobacco [at most, a few cents] a day is considered high wages, and a man will often work for only one" (Jenness and Ballantyne 1920:164). Gold prospectors and miners as well as missionaries typically paid their laborers with stick tobacco, and sometimes it even bought "the precious metal" itself: on Sudest Island in the late 1880s, the local people "had shown no hostility to the miners, who had even made use of them to wash gold; and in one case a native had sold some 4 ounces of gold, value about £15, to a miner for two sticks of tobacco, worth about a halfpenny" (Thomson 1889:514).

A final example pertains to the most priceless commodity of all, at least for missionaries: people's souls. Not all missions adopted the approach, but at least some did (see Hays 1991a for a late-nineteenth-century controversy about the use of tobacco among the London Missionary Society). At Maiva on the south coast in 1897 (Thompson 1900:76),

[t]he teachers naively submitted to us the question of the expediency of following something like the plan which they said was adopted by the Roman Catholic priests. According to their description, it was the practice of the priest to go through the village on Sunday morning with a basket containing a supply of tobacco. He promised a piece of tobacco to every man who attended service, and, in consequence, his ministrations were greatly esteemed by a considerable number of the heathen.

These examples, which could be multiplied many times, illustrate the powerful economic motivation for Europeans to take an active role in the spread of tobacco smoking, though almost certainly not the cultivation of the plant. The prevailing view is well expressed by the administrator, Sir William MacGregor (1894:7), speaking of the Rossel Islanders in 1892: "They have taken kindly to tobacco, and will consequently be willing to trade. Tobacco is not grown on the island."

In addition to being cheap, twist tobacco had many advantages over other European goods. Throughout the Pacific, according to Shineberg (1967:151),

[t]he passion for tobacco suited the trader admirably. It was comparatively cheap trade, it was small and compact to carry and, above all, it was expendable, creating as much demand as it satisfied. After the end of 1849 there was no export cargo destined for the islands that did not include tobacco and many traders did not even bother to take anything else, while others took little besides.

In Papua New Guinea, European involvement began somewhat later, but the same considerations applied. Stick tobacco was more portable and weighed much less than hoop iron or bolts of cloth, it was easily divided into thin slices, and, perhaps most important, it was consumable. Once a demand could be established, given the addictive nature of nicotine, it was one that was constant, and ever-increasing.

In some places establishing a demand was not easy. On Goodenough Island, among the "inverted ethnic jokes which they tell against themselves . . . there is the one about the first men to be offered black twist tobacco by exploring Europeans: thinking it to be pigshit the bewildered recipients threw it away" (Young 1977:76). Thus the appearance of stick tobacco (as well as the sight of smoke pouring out of white mouths and noses) in some cases stimulated little initial interest in sharing such pleasures. One solution, according to the German trader Hernsheim (1983:60) on New Ireland, was to set up "schools for smoking . . . with traders as instructors, in which the new pastime was propagated, so that in a few years time tobacco was the most coveted and indispensable commodity among the natives."

In some places, trade tobacco initially was rejected out of preference for home-grown varieties, but in others, smoking often became what can only be called a passion. On Goodenough Island, where tobacco was unknown in 1891, by 1912, according to the long-resident missionary (Jenness and Ballantyne 1920:163),

[t]wo things appear to the native almost as necessary as his food—betel-nut and tobacco. Abundance of both makes life rosy, their absence robs it of all pleasure. Sometimes the natives assert that they could not live if they were deprived of tobacco. A man would

often come to us and say, "My tobacco was all used up, so I stayed at home in my hamlet. My strength all left me; I existed, and that was all. At last I thought to myself, 'I will go to my father and he will give me some tobacco.'"

And, in the Motu-speaking Port Moresby area, virtually all early European visitors remarked on the "god of the Motuites," as stick tobacco (*kuku* in the Motu language) was called by the adventurer Octavius Stone (1880:89). Visiting missionary Turner (1878:494) put it this way:

There is one foreign habit which the Motu have adopted: this is the use, with them also the abuse, of tobacco. The weed is largely used by men, women, and children; mothers give it to their infants to make them sleep while they are away at their plantations. . . . The natives have become slaves to the weed, and will rather want anything than their smoke, in fact, when food is scarce, they almost live upon tobacco.

Stone (1880:38, 89) adds:

[T]he first words I heard in landing were *kuku, kuku iasi,* repeated several times in an interrogatory voice . . . since then, those words rang constantly in my ears. . . .

Even little babies learn to utter the word *kuku* before *tinana,* "mother." I never knew a people so fearfully fond of this weed. *Kuku* is their god, whom alone they worship and adore. The word *kuku* escapes their lips more than any other in the course of the day, and is ever in their thoughts.

Such reports might lead to the simple judgment that these people became (quickly) addicted to nicotine. But the striking range of variation in response to twist tobacco still needs to be explained. As mentioned earlier, in some areas trade tobacco was rejected out of preference for the locally grown, "native" variety, and in others there was interest but reportedly not to any extraordinary degree. In this regard, revisiting the precolonial distribution of tobacco cultivation and use may be helpful.

At first contact, peoples in virtually all parts of Irian Jaya (with the possible exception of the extreme south coast) and most of Papua New Guinea (excluding the northeastern and southeastern coasts and adjacent island groups) were reported to engage in smoking and, with a few exceptions who depended entirely on trade with neighboring groups, cultivation of the plant. There can be little doubt that tobacco seeds and knowledge regarding their propagation and subsequent use (sometimes as medicines as well as for smoking) had diffused to and nearly throughout New Guinea in post-Columbian times as they had (though perhaps not as rapidly) everywhere else in the world (Goodman 1993).

One of the most important points to be derived from early accounts by Europeans is that where tobacco was grown or used prior to direct Western influence, its use was in almost all cases surrounded with rules. Almost nowhere did recreational smoking exist; instead, primarily because of its purported potency as a psychoactive agent, tobacco smoking was restricted in terms of both eligible parties and contexts: the former, nearly always adult males, and the latter, ritual or symbolic contexts. It is striking that in almost none of these cases (i.e., where tobacco use was long established) was the casual use of tobacco reported, nor were "tobacco fiends" reported upon the introduction of the European product. Rather, the craving for trade tobacco was limited almost entirely to areas where it was new or only recently acquired.

Tobacco's novelty alone cannot account for the worship of the "god of the Motuites," since numerous other European goods did not enjoy such success. While the practical advantages of such items as steel tools and matches seem to have been appreciated nearly everywhere in colonial Papua New Guinea, "craving" or "addiction" are not terms to be found in association with these introductions. But tobacco was a different matter, as has been seen in examples provided above, and indeed Papua New Guinea may only be a specific instance of a worldwide pattern.

In a broader context, Mintz (1987:194-95) has proposed that

> highly desirable substances appear to function differently in areas where they are old (and perhaps less pure) from the way they function in areas where they are newer (and perhaps purer). The sacred tobacco of the Plains Indians did not evoke the use-patterns that have come to typify it in the Western world; whiskey has serious consequences for Europeans, but it wreaked even greater havoc upon American Indians; coca leaves do not do in the Andes what cocaine has done in New York City. Is it possible that substances, even harmful substances, do relatively less harm when the social contexts for their ingestion have had a very long time to take shape?

While information regarding precolonial rates of smoking-related diseases and other harm attributable to tobacco is not available, the current situation in Papua New Guinea is reasonably clear (Marshall 1991). What is also clear is that postcolonial tobacco-use patterns contrast markedly with traditional ones. Small children diving into the sea after bits of tobacco tossed from "The Tobacco Ship," as the London Missionary Society vessel was called in the early days at Port Moresby (Turner 1878:494), would have been unthinkable in most of New Guinea, where they would not have been allowed to smoke, or even handle it. Similarly, judging from early reports, smoking prevalence rates of three-quarters or more of adults in various survey locations in Papua New Guinea in the 1970s and 1980s (Marshall 1991:1332) are very probably a modern phenomenon.

We cannot know, of course, whether tobacco smoking would eventually have become recreational in Papua New Guinea without the assistance of Europeans, any more than we can be certain that it would have completed its apparent path of geographic diffusion. But what seems arguable is that in those areas of Papua New Guinea where tobacco had not yet arrived by the time of significant European presence, the chemical properties of nicotine together with the complete absence of models and rules for its use provided an opportunity for the acceleration of both processes by Westerners.

NOTE

1. Since 1983, I have been engaged in marshalling botanical, ethnographic, historical, and linguistic evidence to reconstruct the introduction and diffusion of tobacco and smoking in New Guinea. This project has been supported primarily by grants awarded by the Rhode Island College Faculty Research Committee. I am grateful to them, and to Sidney Mintz and fellow panelists at the 1998 American Anthropological Association meetings for helpful comments on this small part of the larger study.

TUBER TRANSFORMATIONS: THE IMPACT OF THE SWEET POTATO IN THE INDO-PACIFIC

Richard Scaglion
Todd R. Hooe

One of the greatest enigmas of Pacific prehistory was posed by the discovery in the 1930s of about a million people living at high altitudes in central New Guinea. These people employ intensive systems of tillage, mounding, and drainage to grow sweet potatoes (Ipomoea batatas); *a crop which modern work has unmistakably demonstrated to be of South American origin (Brookfield with Hart 1971:83).*

Like many New World cultivars, the sweet potato has become an important subsistence crop in many Old World societies. In the Indo-Pacific,[1] the sweet potato was adopted by local populations over a long period of time, earlier in some locations but much later in others. The enthusiasm with which this tuber was accepted and its consequent effect on the economies of the region have varied according to ecological, historical, and cultural factors. This essay addresses two important questions related to the diffusion of the sweet potato in the Pacific and Insular Southeast Asia. One is, where did the tuber travel, and when and how did it get there? The other is, what impact did the adoption of sweet potatoes have on local socio-economic systems? In attempting to shed light on these questions, we examine possible routes of introduction of the sweet potato, as well as the distribution and significance of this cultivar for 215 societies of the Indo-Pacific.

The diffusion and adoption of the sweet potato in the tropical and subtropical environments of the Indo-Pacific were facilitated in part by its very nature. It thrives better at higher altitudes and on agriculturally degraded soils than much of the crop inventory previously found throughout the area. As a result, it extended the range of arable land of many peoples of the region without requiring engineering or technological elaboration. In many areas where high-

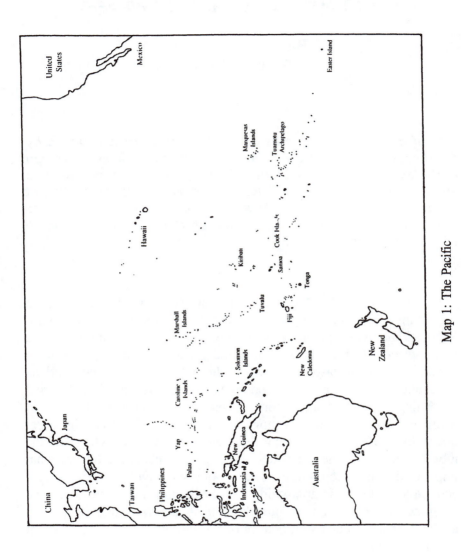

Map 1: The Pacific

altitude land has been available to local populations, the sweet potato has been enthusiastically embraced and has even become a staple crop. Perhaps the clearest example is the New Guinea Highlands, where economic systems based on intensive sweet potato cultivation[2] and the domestication of pigs resulted in the growth of large, stable populations. As Wiessner and Tumu (1998:3) explain for the Enga of the Papua New Guinea Highlands, the sweet potato "permitted people in many areas of Enga to settle more permanently, practice intensive agriculture, expand into higher altitudes, and produce a substantial surplus 'on the hoof' in the form of pigs." The sweet potato thus shifted Highland demographic patterns by making intensive cultivation possible in areas that had been previously underutilized.

SWEET POTATO DIFFUSION IN THE PACIFIC AND INSULAR SOUTHEAST ASIA

According to conventional views, the sweet potato was introduced into Insular Southeast Asia and the Pacific (including New Guinea), via European agency. Swadling (1986:45) summarizes the prevailing orthodoxy as follows:

The sweet potato, now the staple food in the densely populated Highlands [of New Guinea], was introduced here about 300 to 400 years ago from eastern Indonesia. . . . The Spaniards took the sweet potato to Europe and Africa. From there the Portuguese and Spaniards took it to Ambon, Timor and the Moluccas in the 15th and 16th centuries. . . . Papuan pirates, other people from the coast of the Cenderwasih Peninsula paying tribute to Tidore, or Malay traders, may have introduced the sweet potato to coastal areas of Irian Jaya, and from there it was traded to the Highlands.

By this view sweet potatoes were introduced into the western Pacific, including the Highlands of New Guinea, at roughly the same time and place, and by the same agents, as tobacco, described by Hays in this volume. If sweet potatoes were introduced into the New Guinea Highlands only a few hundred years ago, then the development of intensive agricultural systems based on sweet potatoes and pig husbandry, the growth of large, dense populations, and the development of complex ceremonial systems that anthropologists found in the

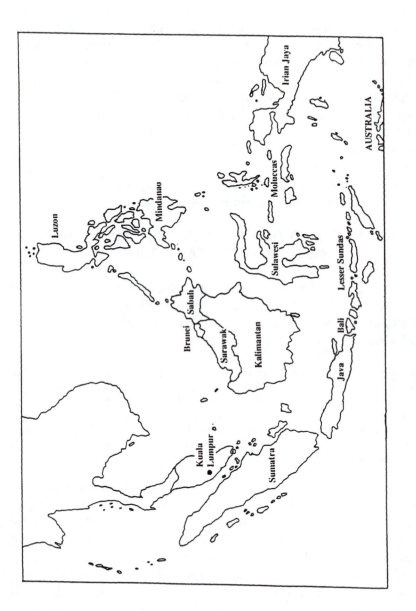

Map 2: Insular Southeast Asia

Highlands during the ethnographic present probably proceeded at an astoundingly rapid pace. Such a view prompted Watson (1965) to write of the possibility of an Ipomoean "revolution" that dramatically transformed Highland economic systems.[3]

The relative speed with which the sweet potato was embraced and local economic systems transformed is critically important. First, it speaks to the rate at which people are able to modify their basic subsistence systems and consequently other aspects of their cultures. Second, if revolutionary changes in Highland economies occurred very rapidly, then the social formations observed by anthropologists during the ethnographic present are perhaps better considered transitory forms rather than stable arrangements. Take, for example, what many introductory anthropology texts call the "big man system" of political organization. In many of these texts (e.g., Hicks and Gwynne 1996:295), certain characteristics of Highland New Guinea leaders are highlighted and presented as paradigmatic of this political type. But if big man systems arose so quickly, they may be regarded as merely a transitory step in the process of developing social stratification, rather than as a discrete political category. Thus the rate at which the sweet potato transformed New Guinea Highland agricultural systems is of broad significance in anthropology.

Recently, new data have come to light that have caused us to re-examine and rethink conventional ideas about the diffusion of the sweet potato into New Guinea. It may be that agricultural changes were not as rapid and dramatic as previously thought. Increasing evidence is being uncovered of quite early remains of sweet potatoes in Polynesia, for example. Excavations at Tangatatau, a large, well-stratified rock shelter in the Cook Islands, produced several specimens of carbonized sweet potato tubers in unquestionably prehistoric contexts. As Hather and Kirch (1991:889, 892-93) put it, "In short, sweet potato remains are represented throughout the deposits, in securely dated contexts that leave no doubt as to the presence of this cultigen during the last millennium of Mangaian prehistory . . . unequivocally establishing the presence of *Ipomoea batatas* in central and eastern Polynesia by around A.D. 1000. . . ." Such findings, coupled with evidence of long-distance trade networks that ultimately link Polynesian societies to those of western Melanesia (see, e.g.,

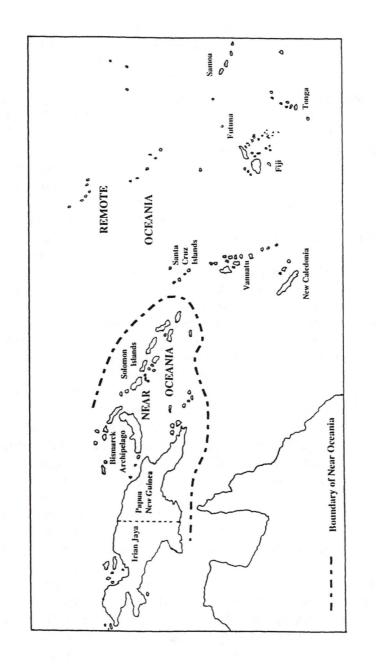

Map 3: Near Oceania

Kirch 1991), lead us to seriously consider the possibility of a prehistoric introduction of sweet potatoes into New Guinea through Polynesia.

Still further evidence comes from a recent study of linguistic terms used for the sweet potato in the Pacific. If sweet potatoes diffused from eastern Indonesia, as conventional models suggest, we might expect some correspondence in terminology between these two regions. But instead, correspondences exist between terms used in eastern New Guinea and those of Polynesia (Scaglion and Soto 1994), lending added support to the hypothesis of a prehistoric introduction through Polynesia.

The implications of a prehistoric introduction of the sweet potato in New Guinea are significant for several reasons. If introduced prehistorically, then the sequence of agricultural intensification in the New Guinea Highlands may have been much longer than conventional models of diffusion suggest.[4] If so, then the political, social, and ceremonial systems observed in the Highlands during the ethnographic present may be less revolutionary, conforming more to the standard textbook accounts of such institutions.

ALTITUDE AND SWEET POTATOES

As previously mentioned, the sweet potato offers important advantages over the essentially tropical food inventory shared by most peoples of Oceania and Insular Southeast Asia. It is quicker to mature and thrives better at higher altitudes than other crops, its rooting system allows for partial harvesting with subsequent development of additional tubers, and it is more tolerant of agriculturally degraded soils (Golson 1982:131). Thus Clarke (1977:161) argued for both extensive and intensive changes in the Highland horticultural base as a result of the introduction of the sweet potato. Cultivation not only could move into higher altitudes and onto poorer soils, but sweet potatoes could also be used as a follow-up crop in a rotational system. Additionally, they provide excellent fodder for pigs, adding to the impetus for intensification (Watson 1977).

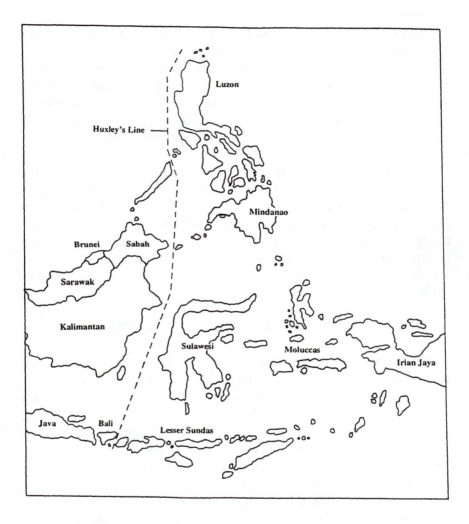

Map 4: Insular Southeast Asia East of Huxley's Line

Given its nature, we might hypothesize that where high-altitude cultivation areas (even poor ones) are available to Southeast Asian and Pacific Islanders, sweet potatoes would be most readily adopted. This hypothesis was tested by examining the significance of the sweet potato according to altitude of available land in both Insular Southeast Asia and the Pacific. For the Pacific (see Map 1), the sample was 135 societies described in the Oceania volume of the *Encyclopedia of World Cultures* (Hays 1991b).[5] It should be noted that this is not a random sample in the statistical sense, but a judgmental one, maximizing geographic representation and ethnographic coverage.

We operationalized our variables as follows. For altitude, we attempted to ascertain the highest elevation at which land is readily available to an ethnographic population, using the *Encyclopedia of World Cultures* Oceania volume. Where information was lacking on altitude, we consulted topographic maps (Rand McNally 1994). Because altitude could be ascertained only roughly, we categorized groups into low- (< 1000 feet), medium- (1000-3000 feet), and high-elevation (> 3000 feet) land available. We then read the ethnographic summaries in an attempt to determine the importance of the sweet potato to the local economy, and classified groups into those where the sweet potato is a major crop, secondary crop, and those where the sweet potato is absent or not reported.[6]

Employing these admittedly rough measures, we nonetheless found a strong association between altitude of available land and the importance of the sweet potato as a staple crop in the Pacific (Table 1). It appears, then, that where high-altitude land has been available to Pacific populations, the sweet potato has been enthusiastically embraced, and its cultivation has been intensive.

To examine the same hypothesis for Insular Southeast Asia (see Map 2), we used a sample of 80 societies from the East and Southeast Asia volume of the *Encyclopedia of World Cultures*[7] (Hockings 1993) and operationalized our variables in the same fashion. No significant correlation was found, however (Table 2). Anticipating a possible argument that the prehistoric presence of sweet potatoes in Polynesia might have confounded the results, we conducted a second pair of analyses by contrasting a subsample of Oceania ("Near Oceania"; see Map 3) with a subsample of Insular Southeast Asia (islands east of

Table 1: Altitude and Significance of the Sweet Potato in the Pacific

	Major Crop	Secondary Crop	Absent/ n.r.	Total
Available Land > 3,000 ft.	27	6	5	38
Available Land 1-3,000 ft.	14	9	14	37
Available Land < 1,000 ft.	6	14	40	60
Total	47	29	59	135

Chi-square=41.49, p≤0.00000, Cramer's V=0.39

Table 2: Altitude and Significance of the Sweet Potato in Insular
Southeast Asia

	Major Crop	Secondary Crop	Absent/ n.r.	Total
Available Land > 3,000 ft.	1	7	23	31
Available Land 1-3,000 ft.	2	6	19	27
Available Land < 1,000 ft.	0	1	21	22
Total	3	14	63	80

Chi-square=5.82, p≤0.22, Cramer's V=0.19

Huxley's line; see Map 4). In both regions, the sweet potato is generally argued to be a historic introduction (see, e.g., Yen 1974), and the cultural and historical environments are more homogeneous than for the broader regions of which they are part. Again, the correlation for Near Oceania is significant ($N=90$, Chi-square$=24.82$, $p \leq 0.00005$, Cramer's $V=0.37$), whereas that for Insular Southeast Asia east of Huxley's line is not ($N=53$, Chi-square$=3.99$, $p \leq 0.41$, Cramer's $V=0.19$).

What explains these variations? Why do the inhabitants of these two regions, with relatively similar environments, display different patterns? First, it should be pointed out that the sweet potato is probably much more prevalent in Insular Southeast Asia than our data might suggest. Given how we operationalized variables, Table 2 illustrates that the sweet potato was unreported for 63 of the 80 societies in the Insular Southeast Asian sample. However, other reports suggest that many of these societies actually do grow sweet potatoes, albeit in small quantities.[8] The fact that its presence went unreported in the encyclopedia's ethnographic descriptions merely demonstrates its relative unimportance as a staple crop in Insular Southeast Asian economies.

Why, in contrast to the Pacific, was this so? One line of argument suggests that the existing crop inventory of Insular Southeast Asia at the time of the introduction of the sweet potato inhibited the role of the tuber in local agricultural systems. As Yen (1974:48-49) points out, the "secondary role" and "subsidiary function" of the sweet potato in the "far eastern Pacific" and "Asiatic islands" is due to the dominance of "annual graminaceous crop plants [cereals] which require stricter cycles of agricultural operations than root crops." Such an argument is problematic for several reasons. First, while it may be true that Old World cereals (e.g., millet and rice) are much more prevalent in many areas of island Southeast Asia, economic systems based on "tubers . . . and fruit or starch-bearing trees . . . are still widespread in remoter parts of Indonesia" (Bellwood 1997:250). Second, the existence of cereal crops did not preclude the enthusiastic adoption of other New World crops in suitable environments throughout the archipelago. For example, maize and cassava have become staple crops in many southern islands of eastern Indonesia (Ellen 1987:38; Fox 1991:248; Monk et al. 1997:700).

We suggest an alternative interpretation of the differing significance of the sweet potato in Insular Southeast Asia and the Pacific based on the premise that, all things being equal, locations showing the most reliance on the cultivar would most likely have had it for the longest period of time. Thus, another interpretation is that the Insular Southeast Asians have not had the sweet potato long enough for it to have become firmly established as an important staple. This is exactly what the model of a prehistoric introduction of the sweet potato from the east, as discussed earlier, predicts.

CONCLUSION

This chapter opened with a question about the diffusion of the sweet potato in the Indo-Pacific. How and when did this cultivar, generally agreed to have been domesticated in Central or South America, find its way into the western Pacific? Polynesians, without a doubt the world's greatest navigators and seafarers at the time, have had the tuber for more than a millennium. It would be surprising if the sweet potato had not been traded westward by Austronesian-speaking peoples long before Magellan stumbled into the area. Our findings suggest the possibility of a prehistoric introduction of the sweet potato in New Guinea, which would allow for much longer-term scenarios for agricultural development and demographic growth in the New Guinea Highlands than are currently being considered.

But whatever the rate at which Highland agricultural systems became transformed, the sweet potato clearly can be a powerful cultivar in high-altitude tropical locales, making possible agricultural intensification and significant demographic and social change. In other parts of the world, intensification has required the engineering of extensive irrigation canals, the use of fertilizer and complex crop rotation systems, or the employment of plow and draft animals.[9] But in the Pacific, the sweet potato extended the range of arable land with very little technological elaboration, making it the right crop at the right place at the right time.

NOTES

1. "Indo-Pacific" here refers to tropical and subtropical islands stretching from Sumatra in western Indonesia to the eastern Polynesian islands of Hawaii and Easter Island. The Indo-Pacific region thus includes Insular Southeast Asia and the islands of Melanesia, Micronesia, and Polynesia (see Maps 1 and 2).

2. According to Brookfield with Hart (1971:112), there are three main techniques utilized for intensive sweet potato cultivation in the New Guinea Highlands: 1) complete tillage, "involving the breaking up and turning the whole soil with digging sticks and hands, and its arrangement in beds with groove drains, or in small mounds"; 2) gridiron ditching, involving "the digging of a close-spaced grid of soil drainage ditches, the soil from which is thrown onto the intervening beds"; and 3) mounding, whereby a "mound site is prepared and the soil thrown out in a ring, which is then filled with sweet-potato vines and other plants; when these have begun to decompose the mound is closed by throwing the soil over it."

3. Watson (1965) argues that the introduction of the sweet potato had revolutionary effects on New Guinea Highland societies, and that aspects of these societies observed at the time of European contact (ca. 1930s) were not well established.

4. Brookfield and White (1968) and others have argued against the idea of an Ipomoean revolution, suggesting that intensive sweet potato cultivation evolved out of pre-existing forms of intensive agriculture. Although Brookfield and White assume that the sweet potato has only been present in the Highlands for 300-400 years, they suggest that sweet potatoes replaced a previous form of intensive agriculture, with taro or yams as the primary crop.

5. We excluded the cultures of Australia from our sample due to the significant differences in environment and subsistence that exist between Australia and the rest of the Pacific. Our sample thus consisted of all cultures listed in the volume for New Guinea (including Irian Jaya), Island Melanesia, Micronesia, and Polynesia.

6. Our criteria for determining the significance of the sweet potato were as follows: if the sweet potato was listed first, second, or third in the description of important crops, we designated it a "major crop"; if it was listed fourth or lower, or was preceded by phrases such as "Other crops grown are . . . " we designated the sweet potato a "secondary crop"; in cases where the sweet potato was not mentioned in the description, we designated it "absent or not reported."

7. This volume covers the cultures of East and Southeast Asia, but we drew our sample areas solely from the cultures of Insular Southeast Asia. Although there are descriptions of 87 cultures for these two, the following seven cultures were dropped from our sample due to insufficient information: Bilaan, Gaddang, Gorontalese, Ibaloi, Itneg, Kalagan, and Kubu.

8. As Boomgaard (1997:16) notes, the sweet potato (along with maize and cassava) has become a ubiquitous food crop throughout Indonesia, although its influence on the environment has hardly been studied.

9. We are grateful to Len Plotnicov for underlining the significance of this fact.

COFFEE: THE MECHANISM OF TRANSITION TO A MONEY ECONOMY[1]

Paula Brown

Coffee planting in the Papua New Guinea Highlands began with land leases for coffee plantations by Australian expatriates in the 1950s and later coffee became a cash crop for Highlands people. When highlanders began to sell their coffee, money became the basis of family expenditure on household goods, clothing, and traditional payments. Differentials in income have developed between Highland people with large coffee land holdings and other economic opportunities and smallholders of the densely populated Simbu and Enga Provinces.

Coffee was seen by the people of the Papua New Guinea Highlands as "money that grows on trees" (Brookfield 1968; Apa 1978). It was the Australian colonial administration, through its district officers and agricultural and cash-crop economic development program, that stimulated this dream and helped them to plant coffee on their own land alongside subsistence food crops. Many highlanders felt that coffee growing and selling would be the key to bringing them out of their precontact, backward, sweet potato subsistence/exchange lifestyle. Between the first contact in 1933 and 1960, rural Chimbu were unfamiliar with money, had no cash income, and there were no stores in the area. With coffee they hoped to be *bisnismen* (entrepreneurs), drive cars and trucks on paved roads, live in Western-style houses, buy their food in shops, and have nice clothes and household goods. In the Chimbu area where I conducted field research in 1958 and later, coffee growing was promoted by Kondom, a popular leader, all over the Highlands (Brown 1995). The area is now Simbu Province, Papua New Guinea.

Now (since 1975) Papua New Guinea is an independent nation, and people are dependent upon money for subsistence needs as well as the ever-changing gift and exchange economy and the commodities of modern life. The Australian administration in the 1950s and 1960s

119

brought roads, schools, medical facilities, and political and economic development institutions leading toward independence. The monetization that followed coffee growing and selling has affected every aspect of life—family and household consumption habits, transportation and mobility, marketing, local trade stores, and the large distributions of wealth that have taken the place of ritual and tribal feasts. It sparked indigenous women's saving and distributions clubs—*wok meri* (Sexton 1986; Warry 1987). Coffee is hardly drunk by rural highlanders; in Papua New Guinea it is a mark of urban sophistication to be taken in towns, hotels, and restaurants. Coffee is not prepared for sale and there are no instant-coffee factories in Papua New Guinea. Highlanders chew betel and smoke cigarettes. They eat and sometimes sell a variety of Pacific and Western crops, new and old; sweet potato, banana, sugar cane, taro, yam, corn, pumpkin, onion, cabbage, potato, and greens.

I will trace the history of coffee in the Highlands as seen locally. My fieldwork began in 1958, just as the first Chimbu coffee was produced and sold. Papua New Guinea Highland people now number about a million, and while their contribution to the world coffee market is tiny (1 per cent), and a small part of their land is devoted to growing coffee, it is of the greatest significance to them.

Coffee was first tried in New Guinea in the 1890s, but the development of coffee first as a cash crop on plantations of Australian expatriates and then of native growers began just before World War II (Sinclair 1995). Trials in the Aiyura research station in the Eastern Highlands in 1937 found high-altitude (Arabica) coffee suitable as an economic crop. Arabica is the variety grown most successfully in the Highlands, the seed derived from trials from the 1930s to the 1940s (Bourke 1986). Some coffee was planted in the early 1940s, and soon after World War II Australian expatriates familiar with the area as government officers and settlers acquired land for plantations in the Eastern and Western Highlands Districts. At the time of this first development there were few airstrips or vehicular roads in the Highlands. Development took off in the 1950s with plantations in Eastern Highlands and Western Highlands Districts (Sinclair 1995). Where land was available, long-term leases for coffee plantation development were supervised by the Australian New Guinea colonial government. Yet in 1959 there was an article expressing concern that Arabica might be overproduced for the world market (Ford 1959). The employment of Highland men on plantations was their introduction to wage labor and to the production of coffee beans. A few enterprising Papua New Guinea highlanders began to plant seedlings around 1950.[2] Plantation laborers with money stimulated development of trade stores, at first owned by expatriates and later by local people. There was a great demand for seed and seedlings among Highland people, and the Department of Agriculture, Stock and Fisheries sent agriculture extension workers to village communities to establish coffee seedling nurseries and encourage planting, leading to cash crop production in this hitherto undeveloped area (Bourke 1986). In many localities, some leaders accepted the seedlings, and the practice spread in a few years when they began to harvest the crop and sell their beans (Apa 1978). Smallholder coffee planting in the Eastern Highlands, Western Highlands, and Chimbu areas preceded that in the Enga and Southern Highlands by some years. Roads to the coast and throughout the Highlands developed as coffee marketing required.

In 1953, the Highland Farmers and Settlers' Association was formed by Australian plantation owners, and the constitution proclaimed their desire to see the Highland people advance. They declared their loyalty to the British throne and the country in which they lived. While it was "multiracial," it was not until 1964 that the Highland Farmers and Settlers' Association formed a Chimbu branch. A bulletin was published that included technical coffee-production information and prices. One quarter-page in 1960 gave information about prices in pidgin English (*tok pisin*), the only language that native coffee producers might possibly read. The leaders traveled to observe coffee production, participated in international coffee discussions, and met to exchange information. They negotiated with Australian and international business interests. Of course, none of this reached the Papua New Guinea highlanders.

The Australian administration saw coffee as the basis of economic development for the region. The Department of Agriculture, Stock and Fisheries promoted coffee planting by local people in the Highlands; agriculture officers prepared coffee seedling nurseries and instructed the people in planting and tending coffee trees. Development of coffee grew rapidly in the Eastern Highlands, where the model of Australian planters and assistance of agricultural officers and extension workers could be followed. Some men developed large holdings (Finney 1973), and rural buying associations were established in the 1960s. On the average, trees per grower ranged from 25 to 441 in the several areas of the Eastern Highlands in 1965 (Donaldson and Good n.d.). Social and gender relations changed little; in 1992 women in the Eastern Highlands were found to have less access to productive assets than have men, to work longer hours, and have a lower return for labor (Overland 1998).

In the Chimbu area the government-sponsored regional leader, Kondom, brought the word to the highlanders. By the mid- to late 1950s there were some group land holdings in which individual men had sections prepared for coffee growing (Brookfield and Brown 1963:49-50). Most of the adult men of the area of central Chimbu had trees. They began bearing about 1959 and reached maturity a few years later, and individual planting has continued. People were told that those who grow coffee will have a lot of money to buy things, trucks will travel on new roads, and growers can hire airplanes to visit other places (Brown 1995:247-51). Many men planted 100 trees or more. When the pioneering bisnismen began to sell coffee and for the first time to buy goods at trade stores, others began to plant coffee and hope for money to spend.

GROWING AND SELLING COFFEE

After the initial clearing, land preparation, and planting of seedlings and shade trees, weeding is the main labor required until harvesting can begin four or five years later. Pruning and replanting are long-term requirements. Some new division of labor developed: men prepare ground, fence, and plant seedlings; women weed; everyone, including children, picks. The coffee bean must be separated from the fruit or "cherry" that surrounds it. Harvesting is followed by pulping, fermenting, and washing, mostly by men. While this processing was at first all done by hand, some labor saving is achieved by pulping machines and buckets or vats. Beans are dried on mats, blankets, or plastic sheets in front of houses before sale. Most

sales are to private buyers who come by truck to roadside market-
places near home areas of the growers. At first only men sold coffee
and decided how to use the money, whether for clothing, food, or
traditional payments (see also Barnes n.d.). By the 1970s I saw
women selling and using money for themselves, children, household
items, school fees, and transportation to town and market (Brown
1988). Interviews in Iabakogl, Chimbu Province, in 1977 and 1978
(Christie 1980) found a wide range in size of subsistence gardens,
coffee gardens, incomes, and expenditure patterns among the families
interviewed. There were men who owned vehicles, coffee buyers,
families with relatives in paid employment who contributed money,
owners of trade stores, sellers of vegetables as well as coffee, and
families who depended mainly on subsistence agriculture.

Several of the first Australian coffee growers were former
administration officers with a concern for fostering the local people's
economic and political development. Beginning in the 1950s, and until
about 1960, plantations dominated coffee production in land area with
productive coffee trees and in production of beans for sale. From
1962-65, production of smallholders and plantations was about equal;
then from 1965 to 1971, smallholder production increased to about
two-thirds of the total (Munnull and Densley n.d.). Now 90 per cent
of coffee is produced by smallholders.

Local men have acquired trucks since the 1960s and dominate the
purchasing and hauling business, in turn selling to larger coffee
factories that further dry and process the beans. These men, and the
investors in plantations and town businesses, are the business elite
now (Finney 1973, 1987).

In 1964, Chimbu got their first experience of participating in a
business enterprise; they founded the Kundiawa Coffee Society (later
called Chimbu Coffee Co-operative), a co-operative that, with
administrative sponsorship and bank loans, collected share capital,
elected a board of directors, and purchased an expatriate-owned
factory. For a time (1965-68), the co-op supported communal
pulping, fermenting, washing, and drying. Some time later, when the
dried coffee beans were sold to the co-op, money came to the local
processing group and returns were divided according to the quantity
of cherry each member brought in. About 40 per cent of coffee

growers (17,700 families) became members. It was the largest co-operative in New Guinea. For a few years co-operative members enthusiastically joined together to improve processing and sell to the co-op. However, management and fiscal problems arose, as well as disputes about purchasing and hauling practice. Share payments declined. Private buyers who offered immediate payment to individuals became competitive; the co-op declined, and finally failed (Hide, pers. comm.).

The coffee is purchased at roadsides, and the largest numbers of growers live and sell coffee in the areas nearest to the Highlands highway and feeder roads. It may then be sold to coffee factories, which dry the beans, remove parchment, and haul bags by truck to the coast, where it is shipped overseas. Most New Guinea coffee goes to Australia and Germany. Coffee from Papua New Guinea is subject to the same price fluctuations as coffee produced elsewhere, so when there is a poor crop in Brazil, prices rise internationally; then they may drop. The highlanders have never understood international price fluctuations, but they react by picking and selling more from their trees in high-price years and less when the price drops. Coffee ripens and is picked, processed, and sold mainly over a short period of three or four months. The "flush" (May to August) is celebrated with household purchases of food and goods, food and drinking parties, payments, gambling, marriage arrangements, and a decline in subsistence activities. For some of the people with large coffee holdings in the Eastern and Western Highlands, and some buyers and others who profit in the coffee flush period, subsistence gardening and traditional home activities have declined as the family became dependent on money for purchases of all household necessities.

Planting was done mostly on the scattered private land holdings of Chimbu families. It was also found that maintenance of trees and plants, and the availability and suitability of land (soil, moisture, altitude) varied. The land of Chimbu families is divided among several plots in different sections of clan territory, and frequently coffee was planted in several very small plots (Warry 1987; Howlett et al. 1976). In the area of central Chimbu that we studied and measured, coffee planting grew from 0.01 ha/capita in 1958 to 0.06 ha/capita in 1967 (Brookfield 1973:156). Climate and growing conditions, roads, and marketing opportunities have affected the distribution of people, land use, and social differentiation in the Highlands area (Brookfield 1968, 1973, 1996; Brown 1995). Settlement has changed: within Chimbu, coffee opportunities center on the highway. People have built their houses as close to the highway as they could, and many people with no land where coffee can grow, or land very distant from the highway, have resettled at other sites or sought work in towns (Rambo 1993). This is reflected also in the number of coffee trees per capita, which varies from none to 95 in the several areas within Simbu Province (Howlett et al. 1976:224). Smallholding is variable: the average in Kapanara, Eastern Highlands, was 0.045 ha/capita (Grossman 1984:185) but less in many other areas. Estimates of coffee income, number of trees, and planted area per capita are based on surveys that found the areas planted to coffee ranged from 0.01 to 0.25 ha/capita, with varying densities of trees as well as population densities and land in food crops (Wohlt and Goie 1986). In those areas of Simbu Province that are unfavorable to coffee growing, emigration to work in towns has become common.

CASH AND CONSEQUENCES

Furthermore, abundance of land in the Eastern Highlands and Western Highlands allowed selling land for plantation development by Australian expatriates, while because of high population density and shortage of land in Chimbu and Enga the Australian administration did not allow land alienation for plantations; only small holdings by families were permitted. Since the 1970s, Eastern and Western Highland people have acquired many former plantations and have also expanded planting coffee on family land. In 1987 one young Eastern Highlands teacher's college student showed me his coffee holdings and available land for expansion; he said he could earn far more in four months of coffee production than he would ever earn as a teacher. In contrast, many Chimbu families who cannot acquire land for planting coffee find it hard to pay their children's school fees and cannot afford to send them to high school or any higher education that might lead to a job.

Chimbu has been transformed from a subsistence household economy, in which all food and basic needs of clothing, housing, tools, and ritual objects were obtained by home labor, hunting, gathering, cultivation, and local trade, to a money economy. For the Chimbu smallholder, who had no money and never purchased anything from a trade store until he had a coffee crop to sell, coffee became the chief source of household income, used for store foods (rice, tinned meat, tinned fish, sweets, soft drinks), small celebrations, beer, clothing, tools, and building materials. In the 1950s serious infant and child malnutrition was found in Chimbu, and an infant health program demonstrated peanut, banana, and other solid foods for infant feeding. By the 1970s native foods were frequently supplemented with store purchases, and infant malnutrition almost disappeared (Harvey and Heywood 1983). Trade stores in Chuave, Simbu Province, stocked food, soft drinks, tobacco, clothes, tools, household goods, kerosene, and soap in 1980. Household incomes ranged somewhere around an average of 226 Kina (approximately $220), and there was some economic stratification (Warry 1987). Roadside produce markets add some occasional income year round and are also sources of foods and goods.

The income also supports the largesse of candidates for political office, and there are now great discrepancies in wealth and standard of living in the Highlands. While smallholders in Chimbu, Enga, and the Southern Highlands have few modern houses and no running water or electricity, some Western and Eastern Highland people have been able to acquire and develop plantations, run trucks to buy and transport coffee, and support political candidates lavishly. I saw the beginning of stratification in the 1980s. Coffee growing, coffee processing, buying, shipping, and selling are the chief businesses of Papua New Guinea Highland people, from smallholders to large processing factories and shipping companies. It is the foundation of corporations involved in banking, retail, and wholesale business (Finney 1973, 1987). It is also deeply involved in politics, from the donation of small hand-operated pulpers from a Papua New Guinea Parliament minister's funds to financing a political campaign. Money is now essential to everyday life and all Chimbu gifts and exchange activities are based upon money and purchased goods and foodstuffs.

After independence in 1975, most of the expatriate settlers, government officers, and coffee growers returned to Australia, and plantations have been sold or leased back to the original land-owning groups. From 1974-1980 the government sponsored a twenty-hectare scheme whereby plots were acquired to be managed by local community groups (Sinclair 1995). Papua New Guinea business development companies took over rural and urban land and plantations, creating corporations with a few wealthy owners. The new PNG-owned business corporations often employ Australian managers. In recent years disputes between land owners, plantation lease holders, large coffee factory processors, haulers, and sellers to international markets have often become violent, so that many plantation operators and families have left. Government-sponsored coffee industry boards have been opposed by business interests, and political factions are involved in the coffee industry as land owners, marketers, and processors (Hide, pers. comm.; Sinclair 1995). Today, large business interests and the government-sponsored Coffee Industry Corporation are sometimes opposed on questions of policy and marketing. The industry is not immune to Papua New Guinea's widespread problems of crime and conflict.

Coffee is the largest export crop of Papua New Guinea. Variation in coffee production is linked not only to conditions in the Papua New Guinea Highlands but, more important, to prices for coffee on world markets (Kuimbakul 1994). Coffee production and sales reports from year to year reflect both local conditions and world prices. In 1976-77, due to low yields in other coffee-producing areas, coffee production soared and incomes rose. Prices fell after 1977 and production dropped. Blocks and plantations produced between 250,000 and 310,000 bags (60-kg bags) of green bean in the years 1987 to 1994; smallholder production was 557,000 to 960,000 in this period. Production continued to increase to 1.2 million bags in 1997.

In a recent report, a coffee industry spokesman said coffee would continue to be the main provider of income and employment for Simbu Province, which produces about 8.5 per cent of the country's total production. There are over 40,000 smallholder coffee growers in Chimbu. In the 1996-1997 coffee season, the province produced 89,547 bags. The coffee produced by the province earned more than

K23 million in foreign exchange. Chimbu provincial officials and coffee industry extension services have begun to provide training, credit services, technical information, and advisory service to coffee growers which, it is hoped, will boost total production.

Certainly, local and international conditions affect coffee production, sales, prices, and incomes in Papua New Guinea, and most of these are not under the peoples' control. In 1997 *el niño*-related drought and fires destroyed trees; in 1998 an increase in coffee production was reported. Just as this essay was written, in 1998, the effect of Hurricane Mitch on Central America was expected to reduce coffee production there, and that would favor Papua New Guinea coffee exports and prices. Currency has been devalued, increasing coffee production while raising prices of imported goods.

What has happened to the great expectations of Chimbu in 1960? Chimbu are no longer isolated, but involved in the economy and politics of Papua New Guinea. With independence has come a decline in law and order, with fewer government officers to help or interpret. Schools, churches, and clinics are in every area. There are more educated Chimbu, some individual business successes, and some few Chimbu live in towns with urban amenities, but there is not much improvement in standard of living for most rural people. A growing land shortage limits land for food and expansion of coffee as a cash crop. All Chimbu are familiar with the things that money can buy, and many have traveled to the cities of Papua New Guinea by truck, car, or plane. Most continue to eat sweet potatoes and cultivated vegetables, rarely pork, but purchase some food and beverages. They also depend in part upon the wage income of family members working in the province or outside.

The Papua New Guinea government-supported Coffee Industry Corporation's general manager for extension services, Jon Yogiyo, highlighted the problems in a brief to top management. "Due to deteriorating infrastructure, law and order problem, lack of basic services, high cost of inputs and transport, growers in Chimbu are having a tough time," he said (Korugl-Kumugl 1998). While Highland incomes that depend on coffee will surely continue to fluctuate, Papua New Guinea has taken a turn now toward resource exploitation (logging, mining), in which the densely settled agricultural Highlands area will be little involved. That is where it is going. Yet the Asian financial crisis of 1998 seems to have greatly reduced logging activities for a time and may have some beneficial environmental effect.

Uncertain is the future.

NOTES

1.   This essay was written from a background of 30 years of fieldwork and great hospitality and help from friends in Simbu Province. Much of the fieldwork was conducted in collaboration with Harold Brookfield and I owe a great deal to his measures and insights on Chimbu coffee and land use. I am also grateful to Robin Hide and Dan Jorgensen for providing me with data and reports, published and unpublished.
2.   With the help of Australian Jim Taylor, Baito Heiro started a plantation and became a wealthy coffee producer in the 1950s (Finney 1973:55; Donaldson and Good n.d.:145).

FINAL WORDS[1]

Sidney W. Mintz

It will not have escaped careful readers that nearly all of these diverse essays deal with plants (and the foods that come from them) originating in the New World. Papayas and pineapples, peppers both hot and sweet, peanuts and cashews, sweetsops and soursops, potatoes and sweet potatoes are only a few of the products of Native American cultivating genius. Domesticated by the descendants of the first immigrants, who had come from Asia millennia before those Europeans seeking Asia were to stumble upon the Americas, these foods mark the ancient division into the Old and New World culture spheres. With only two major exceptions, the contributions in this collection center on plants and foods that were carried eastward to Africa and Europe—and in some cases to Asia as well—across the Atlantic, toward the rising sun.

In his splendid *The Columbian Exchange* (1972), Alfred Crosby enlightened countless readers who had not been invited before to think seriously about the transoceanic movement of plants and animals, particularly from the New World to Europe. Since that time, the much-heralded five-hundredth anniversary of the Discovery (as it is rather quaintly called) brought the news to the world again: maize and quinoa, lima beans and string beans, tomatoes and Jerusalem artichokes—a cornucopia of valuable and important foods and food sources were domesticated in the Americas (see, for example, Viola and Margolis 1991).

The exceptions discussed in the present collection are the sweet potato (*Ipomoea batatas*), which may indeed have reached Africa by being carried eastward from the New World but is discussed here in terms of its spread to insular Southeast Asia and Melanesia, in that instance by a westward, trans-Pacific movement; and sugar cane (*Saccharum officinarum*), the world's major source of sucrose, an Old World domesticate. Sugar cane was brought to the New World by Columbus and, since it had been domesticated in New Guinea, by 1493, when it arrived in the Americas, it had nearly girdled the globe.

What the other essays in this collection make clear is the enormous importance of the new American foods for the Old World, where they served to supplement or supplant ancient comestibles (sometimes in the form of fodder) and changed the character and tempo of local life across Europe and large parts of Asia and Africa. The potato, *Solanum tuberosum,* is a special symbol of that process, since it remade the colonial character of Irish life and, by the eventually disastrous effects upon the Irish people, changed as well the demography of the many other places to which the Irish fled. But as these essays show, there is no end of instances where the introduction of a new food has economic, social, and even political effects, unanticipated and unheralded, often of great importance.

Such studies are consistent with the hopes of the first scientific anthropologists, moving from an age of myth and imagination into an era of fieldwork and verification. Visiting and observing peoples who lived by cultivation and by herding, anthropologists thrust themselves into the hurly-burly of daily life in societies no longer dependent on hunting and gathering, where people were managing to extract their livelihoods by considerable effort, exploiting domesticated organisms. Domestication involves the mastery by humankind of the diet, movement, territory, and above all the sexuality of other living things. In each such instance, humans and the living things they controlled and lived by were intertwined in daily life, in experience, and in human thought. Nor should it be missed, in this era of the rediscovery of material culture, that a cultivated plant or animal is as much an artifact of human ingenuity as any hoe, arrow straightener, or canoe. Our predecessors in the field (working, for example, with Inuit, Nuer, and Trobriand Islanders) had a lively awareness of this cultural character of the animate world by virtue of their daily contact, often under extremely difficult field conditions, with the people, and with their plants and animals.

Those anthropologists and their predecessors sought to record all aspects of human behavioral variety around the globe, and the distribution of all aspects of culture, including, very importantly, modes of subsistence, domesticated plants and animals, techniques of cultivation, processing, and food use. They saw these aspects of culture as evidence of human ingenuity; they observed how delicately basic food-getting techniques could be integrated with local environments, and made into subsistence possibilities by purposeful human effort—by intelligent, scientific endeavor. Science without books; science without laboratories; science without the more elaborate goals of science; yet science all the same.

Clark Wissler, who had learned from Otis T. Mason the concept of "ethnic environments," put his own ideas together with Mason's in contriving a culture-areas scheme for the Americas. He based his culture areas on what he called "food areas": a salmon area, an acorn area, a bison area, and so on. Alfred Louis Kroeber, going a big step further, improved on Wissler's ideas in a sophisticated manner in his book, *Cultural and Natural Areas of Native North America*—a book which, unfortunately, no one reads any longer. Here one sees the integration of productive technique and what the local environment makes possible, at some specific technological and social level, for each of the major areas of the northern hemisphere of the Americas.[2]

There was, among scholars such as Mason, Wissler, and Kroeber, ample recognition of the importance of the study of food. To be sure, with some notable exceptions there was probably not quite enough interest in cooking; but there was interest in the study of food. Inherently interdisciplinary questions posed by these scholars were linked to the expertise needed to answer them; what they wanted to understand and to explain regularly exceeded the limits of anthropology as it was then known. To be sure, the skills of the linguist, the physical anthropologist, the archaeologist, and the cultural anthropologist often meshed in addressing a particular question about food origins, food practices, and food beliefs. But the skills of palaeobotanists, palynologists, agronomists, nutritionists, and even cooks also mattered to the resolution of some issues.

Scholars such as Oakes Ames at Harvard, Carl Ortwin Sauer at Berkeley, Edgar Anderson at the Missouri Botanical Garden, and Berthold Laufer at the Chicago Field Museum hobnobbed with anthropologists; and anthropologists hobnobbed with them, because they felt their interests were common and they had something to teach each other.[3]

In view of that past (which I do not mean to idealize or simplify) it is interesting to observe in recent decades some new trends that might well stimulate studies of the kind that comprise this collection. Even though to my knowledge these new trends are not yet linked in any theoretically fulfilling way with studies of plant diffusion, their potential link is real.

I believe that two of these innovative developments are rather broader than anthropology itself. The first such is a direct result of the shift in the study focus from so-called primitive, supposedly self-contained societies, thought to be explainable in terms of themselves, to large, complex societies, which appear to be more integrated into a world economy. In those earlier cases, such as the Trobriand Islanders or the Tikopians, production and consumption were viewed as two sides of a single system, and consumption was not so much studied in terms of itself but in its relationship with production.

The new trend is to study consumption as separate from production; in large measure it is studied in its function as ideologically normative, to some extent divorced from production and, at times, even from class. I am not convinced that the ideologically normative function of consumption is actually very significant. It is, I think, a version of ideological solidarity that one might refer to these days as the "Honk if you've also got a Volvo" complex. The supposedly significant sociological consequences of people consuming the same sorts of goods at the same level are not yet very clear to me, perhaps because I do not grasp how their behavior, individually or collectively, need have any significant effect in terms of power on the producers. Not buying a particular sort of CD player or automobile will surely make its producers nervous; they have to create a new model and pay smaller dividends to their stockholders. But could this be what is meant by the power of the consumer?

The second such trend has to do with food itself and, even more, with eating. It is traceable in some degree to a lengthy period of increasing affluence in the West, and particularly in the United States. In a society such as the United States, marked by ever-increasing discrimination in food preferences and ever-declining competence in average cooking skills, the raging interest in eating in an ever more refined and exotic manner should not really surprise anybody. But both consumption studies and food studies have developed in recent decades without serious attention to linking the study of consumption to the study of food, or to linking both spheres, food and consumption, to the kinds of concerns expressed here. As a consequence, I think, there remains a conceptual task that has to be addressed by people with these interests if we want to unite these three cognate, but conceptually not clearly linked, subjects: food studies, consumption studies, and studies of the history of the diffusion of food plants and processing techniques.

It is for these reasons that I find the essays here both encouraging and enlightening. All of the contributions deal with diffusion in one or another way, but the particular perspectives differ substantially. Brown on coffee in Papua New Guinea, Hays on tobacco there, and Holtzman on cultivated plants among the Samburu deal with varied forms of imperialist administrative imposition and how it has affected life "on the ground." Roberts on maize in Africa and Frechione on manioc (cassava) in Africa deal with the diffusion of specific plants into new areas, where the mechanics of diffusion differ, and the consequences are somewhat unexpected. Here crops are not so much imposed as imperfectly and unevenly accepted, possibly with some potentially sinister consequences, in the case of the people of the Keiyo district. The presence of cretinism among manioc eaters who are eating tubers that have not been adequately processed is another warning of what happens when diffusion is incomplete. Perhaps similar, the "Pellagra Vector," as I think of it, which left its effects in North America and southern Europe, was a direct consequence of the failure to use lime to soften corn kernels—a nutritionally essential process that had typified indigenous maize use among Native Americans. This imperfect transmission of processing parallels the spread of bitter manioc without those proper detoxifying techniques that should have accompanied it.

Brandes on the potato/tomato and Susan Tax Freeman on capsicums deal with comparative cases of the diffusion of exotics within Europe itself; though, as Freeman points out, both Spain and Hungary are themselves somewhat marginal to Europe, if one conceptualizes it narrowly. Brandes, like Freeman, is interested in food-related imagery and in consumer resistance or reluctance when confronted with new foods.

Scaglion and Hooe engage a historical issue which they attempt to illuminate by seeking a correlation between available Highland land for cultivation and the length of use of the sweet potato (*Ipomoea batatas*). Dodds tackles a problem that is ecological but also historical in dealing with long-term effects of crop changes upon Miskito life. And Weismantel and Mintz roam widely in considering the migratory history of a single source of sweetness.

Plotnicov has admirably summarized this highly diverse body of research, but a couple of more general comments may be useful. Anyone who read the great Soviet botanist Nikolai Vavilov, who ended his days in a Stalin concentration camp, or who read Oakes Ames on economic annuals, or Carl Sauer's papers half a century ago on agriculture in the Americas and the origins of domestication, would have no trouble at all in linking their work to what were then current anthropological concerns, or to what are the concerns in this volume. Anthropologists of that era recognized the enormous impact of New World cultivars on the Old World and the gains and losses to the New World that were represented by the diffusion of Old World plants and animals to the New. There was a lively interest in those days in the possibly pre-Columbian trans-Pacific diffusion of *Ipomoea batatas;* provocative debates about black-boned chickens in southern South America to settle the possibility of pre-Columbian diffusion or independent domestication of chickens in the New World; and other controversies. There were some ingenious reflections on the origins and domestication of cassava. In short, studies of the historical distribution of cultural materials, including plants and animals, across the globe were considered anthropologically relevant and worthy of serious attention.

In those days consumption was seen in its primary relationship with production—as mediated through a social system to be studied. That is, consumption could be studied as the other face of production. And food, too, was studied by anthropologists, though primarily in its relationship to the social system and not so much on its own terms. If one reads, for instance, Audrey Richards's *Land, Labour, and Diet in Northern Rhodesia* (which I think may be the best anthropological monograph on food ever written), one sees that it remains to this day a work of lively and intellectually illuminating character.

But all or nearly all of that work typically dealt with problems that were primarily historical, or else that lay within societies whose integration within the world economy was partial or defective or minor, thereby avoiding many of the very problems with which the contributors to this volume are struggling. So it should not be thought that what I am longing for here is some kind of Arcadian epoch now past.

What may be worthwhile pointing out is that our students are perhaps not getting as much these days as they should be getting about the need for interdisciplinary co-operation—not only between anthropologists and other disciplines, but also within anthropology, where despite the kind of reach exemplified by, say, the research of archaeologist Bruce Smith and others, our once at least minimally coherent subfields continue to drift ever farther apart.

It seems to me likely that our serious efforts to bring together food studies, consumption studies, and problems in the history of the diffusion of cultivated plants ought to be redoubled. I find it discouraging that so much energy could have been invested in recent years in reinventing the study of material culture without it being clearly understood, for example, that domesticated plants and animals are among the most important items of material culture that our species has ever fashioned. Reconstructing a unified anthropology on a material basis would be a service to our ancestors. But even more, it could be a service to our students, some of whom may be wondering where, in the anthropology of the modern world, everything material that is not connected to art has disappeared to. Recognition of the material basis of human existence, as recorded through ethnography, and the willingness to consider adaptation, among other things, as changeable (and even possibly improvable under some circumstances) have long been part of anthropology's perspective. What these contributions suggest is that studies of the history of material culture, diffusion, and human ingenuity still possess a lively relevance to the field of anthropology.

NOTES

1. The writer thanks Leonard Plotnicov and William Sturtevant for valuable assistance and advice. Unfortunately, they cannot be blamed for any of the mistakes.

2. Julian Steward, Kroeber's student, carried these ideas farther yet in his theory of cultural ecology.

3. I am reminded of a remark made to me at the 1998 American Anthropological Association annual meetings at which these papers were first delivered. "Do you realize," said my fellow diner, "that three or four thousand people who have come to these meetings, and who describe the meetings as anthropological and themselves as anthropologists, for the larger part no longer have anything to say to each other?"

BIBLIOGRAPHY

Achaya, K. T. 1994. Indian Food: A Historical Companion. Delhi.

Acland, J. D. 1986. East African Crops. Essex.

Algar, A. E. 1985. The Complete Book of Turkish Cooking. London.

Amin, M. 1987. The Last of the Maasai. London.

Andrews, J. 1984. Peppers: The Domesticated Capsicums. Austin.

Anochili, B. C. 1984. Food Crop Production. Nairobi.

Apa, M. A. 1978. Coffee Growing in Kupau Village, Simbu Province. History of Agriculture Working Paper no. 13. Port Moresby.

Arhem, K. 1987. Meat, Milk and Blood: Diet as Cultural Code among the Pastoral Masai. Upsala.

Babaleye, T. 1996. Cassava, Africa's Food Security Crop. CGIAR News 3(1):http://www.worldbank.org/html/cgiar/newsletter/Mar96/4cas2. htm].

Baksh, M. 1995. Changes in Machiguenga Quality of Life. Indigenous Peoples and the Future of Amazonia: An Ecological Anthropology of an Endangered World, ed. L. E. Sponsel, pp. 187-205. Tucson.

Barlett, P. F. 1980. Adaptive Strategies in Peasant Agricultural Production. Annual Review of Anthropology 9:545-73.

Barnes, H. n.d. Women in Highlands Agricultural Production. A Time to Plant and a Time to Uproot, eds. D. Denoon and C. Snowden, pp. 265-84. Port Moresby.

Barrera, Fr. J. L. 1996. 100 recetas de Fray Juan de Guadalupe. Madrid.

Beadle, G. W. 1979. The Origin of Zea Mays. Origins of Agriculture, ed. C. A. Reed, pp. 615-35. The Hague.

Beckerman, S. 1987. Swidden in Amazonia and the Amazon Rim. Comparative Farming Systems, eds. B. L. Turner, II, and S. B. Brush, pp. 55-94. New York.

———— 1993. Major Patterns in Indigenous Amazonia Subsistence. Tropical Forests, People, and Food: Biocultural Interactions and Applications to Development, eds. C. M. Hladik, A. Hladik, O. F. Linares, H. Pagezy, A. Semple, and M. Hadley, pp. 411-24. Paris.

Behrens, C. 1986. The Cultural Ecology of Dietary Change Accompanying Changing Activity Patterns among the Shipibo. Human Ecology 14:367-96.

Bellwood, P. 1997. Prehistory of the Indo-Malaysian Archipelago. Honolulu.

Bevan, T. F. 1890. Toil, Travel, and Discovery in British New Guinea. London.

Boomgaard, P. 1997. Introducing Environmental Histories in Indonesia. Paper Landscapes: Explorations in the Environmental History of Indonesia, eds. P. Boomgaard, F. Colombijn, and D. Henley, pp. 1-26. Leiden.

Boserup, E. 1966. The Conditions of Agricultural Growth: The Economics of Agrarian Change under Population Pressure. Chicago.

Bourdoux, P., F. Delange, M. Gerard, M. Mafuta, A. Hanson, and A. M. Ermans. 1980a. Antithyroid Action of Cassava in Humans. Role of

Cassava in the Etiology of Endemic Goitre and Cretinism, eds. A. M. Ermans, N. M. Mbulamoko, F. Delange, and R. Ahluwalia, pp. 61-68. Ottowa.

Bourdoux, P., M. Mafuta, A. Hanson, and A. M. Ermans. 1980b. Cassava Toxicity: The Role of Linamarin. Role of Cassava in the Etiology of Endemic Goitre and Cretinism, eds. A. M. Ermans, N. M. Mbulamoko, F. Delange, and R. Ahluwalia, pp. 15-27. Ottawa.

Bourke, R. M. 1986. Village Coffee in the Eastern Highlands of Papua New Guinea. The Journal of Pacific History 21:100-03.

Bowles, B. D. 1979. Underdevelopment in Agriculture in Colonial Kenya: Some Ecological and Dietary Aspects. Ecology and History in East Africa, ed. B. A. Ogot, pp. 195-215. Nairobi.

Bradburd, D., and W. Jankowiak. 1999. Getting Hooked on the World Market: Drug Foods, Desire, and Capitalist Expansion. Unpublished ms.

Brandes, S. 1992. Maize as a Culinary Mystery. Ethnology 31:331-36.

Brookfield, H. 1968. The Money that Grows on Trees. Australian Geographical Studies 6:97-119.

———— 1973. Full Circle in Chimbu: A Study of Trends and Cycles. The Pacific in Transition: Geographical Perspectives on Adaptation and Change, ed. H. Brookfield, pp. 127-60. London.

———— 1996. Untying the Chimbu Circle: An Essay in and on Insight. Work in Progress: Essays in Honour of Paula Brown Glick, eds. H. Levine and A. Ploeg, pp. 63-84. Frankfurt am Main.

Brookfield, H. C., and P. Brown. 1963. Struggle for Land. Melbourne.

Brookfield, H. C., with D. Hart. 1971. Melanesia: A Geographical Interpretation of an Island World. London.

Brookfield, H. C., and J. P. White. 1968. Revolution or Evolution in the Prehistory of the New Guinea Highlands: A Seminar Report. Ethnology 7:43-52.

Brown, P. 1988. Gender and Social Change: New Forms of Independence for Simbu Women. Oceania 59:123-42.

———— 1995. Beyond a Mountain Valley: The Simbu of Papua New Guinea. Honolulu.

Buechler, H., and J.-M. Buechler. 1996. The World of Sofía Velásquez: The Autobiography of a Bolivian Market Vendor. New York.

Byerlee, D., and C. K. Eicher (eds.). 1997. Africa's Emerging Maize Revolution. Boulder.

Byerlee, D., and P. W. Heisey. 1997. Evolution of the African Maize Economy. Africa's Emerging Maize Revolution, eds. D. Byerlee and C. K. Eicher, pp. 9-24. Boulder.

Carrera Colin, J. 1981. Apuntes para una investigación etnohistórica de los cacicazgos del corregimiento de Latacunga S.S. XVI y VXII. Cultura (Quito) 4(11):129-79.

Cattle, D. J. 1977. Nutritional Security and the Strategy of Purchasing: The Coastal Miskito Indians, Eastern Nicaragua. Ph.D. dissertation, University of New Mexico. Albuquerque.

Christie, M. 1980. Report no. 3. Changing Consumer Behavior in Papua New Guinea: Its Social and Ecological Implications. Canberra.

Clarke, W. C. 1977. A Change of Subsistence Staple in Prehistoric New Guinea. Proceedings of the Third Symposium of the International Society for Tropical Root Crops, ed. C. L. A. Leaky, pp. 159-63. Ibadan.

Cock, J. H. 1985. Cassava: New Potential for a Neglected Crop. Boulder.

Coe, S. D. 1994. America's First Cuisines. Austin.

Cohen, R. (ed.) 1988. Satisfying Africa's Food Needs: Food Production and Commercialization in African Agriculture. Boulder.

Colony and Protectorate of Kenya. 1921. Samburu District Annual Reports.

————— 1928. Samburu District Annual Reports.

————— 1943. Samburu District Annual Reports.

————— 1947. Samburu District Annual Reports.

————— 1950. Samburu District Annual Reports.

————— 1951. Samburu District Annual Reports.

Conzemius, E. 1929. Notes on the Miskito and Sumu Languages of Eastern Nicaragua. International Journal of American Linguistics 5:57-115.

————— 1932. Ethnographical Survey of the Miskito and Sumu Indians of Honduras and Nicaragua. Washington DC.

Covarrubias, S. de. 1989 (1611). Tesoro de la Lengua Castellana o Española, ed. M. de Riquer. Barcelona.

Crosby, A. W., Jr. 1972. The Columbian Exchange: Biological and Cultural Consequences of 1492. Westport CT.

Delange, F., C. H. Thilly, and A. M. Ermans. 1980. Endemic Goitre in Kivua Area, Africa: Focus on Cassava. Role of Cassava in the Etiology of Endemic Goitre and Cretinism, eds. A. M Ermans, N. M. Mbulamoko, F. Delange, and R. Ahluwalia, pp. 29-36. Ottowa.

Denevan, W. M. 1992. The Pristine Myth: The Landscape of the Americas in 1492. Annals of the Association of American Geographers 82(3):369-85.

Denevan, W. M., and C. Padoch (eds.). 1987. Swidden-Fallow Agroforestry in the Peruvian Amazon. Advances in Economic Botany, Vol. 5. New York.

DeWitt, D., and P. W. Bosland. 1996. Peppers of the World: An Identification Guide. Berkeley.

Diamond, J. 1997. Guns, Germs, and Steel: The Fates of Societies. New York.

Dodds, D. J. 1994. The Ecological and Social Sustainability of Miskito Subsistence in the Río Plátano Biosphere Reserve, Honduras: The Cultural Ecology of Swidden Horticulturalists in a Protected Area. Ph.D. dissertation, University of California. Los Angeles.

―――― 1998. Lobster in the Rain Forest: The Political Ecology of Miskito Wage Labor and Agricultural Deforestation. Journal of Political Ecology 5:83-108.

Dole, G. E. 1960. Techniques of Preparing Manioc Flour as a Key to Culture History in Tropical America. Men and Cultures: Selected Papers of the Fifth International Congress of Anthropological and Ethnological Sciences, 1956, ed. A. F. C. Wallace, pp. 241-48. Philadelphia.

―――― 1994. The Use of Manioc among the Kuikuru: Some Interpretations. The Nature and Status of Ethnobotany, ed. R. I. Ford, pp. 217-47. Ann Arbor.

Donaldson, M., and K. Good. n.d. The Eastern Highlands: Coffee and Class. A Time to Plant and a Time to Uproot, eds. D. Denoon and C. Snowden, pp. 143-70. Port Moresby.

Dufour, D. L. 1989. Effectiveness of Cassava Detoxification Techniques Used by Indigenous Peoples in Northwest Amazonia. Interciencia 14(2):88-91.

―――― 1993. The Bitter Is Sweet: A Case Study of Bitter Cassava (Manihot esculenta) Use in Amazonia. Tropical Forests, People and Food: Biocultural Interactions and Applications to Development, eds. C. M. Hladik, A. Hladik, O. F. Linares, H. Pagezy, A. Semple, and M. Hadley, pp. 575-88. Paris.

―――― 1995. A Closer Look at the Nutritional Implications of Bitter Cassava Use. Indigenous Peoples and the Future of Amazonia: An Ecological Anthropology of an Endangered World, ed. L. E. Sponsel, pp. 149-65. Tucson.

Dunn, O., and J. E. Kelley, Jr. (eds.) 1988. The *Diario* of Christopher Columbus's First Voyage to America, 1492-1493, Abstracted by Fray Bartolomé de las Casas, transl. O. Dunn and J. E. Kelley, Jr. Norman.

Eicher, C. K., and D. Byerlee. 1997. Accelerating Maize Production: Synthesis. Africa's Emerging Maize Revolution, eds. D. Byerlee and C. K. Eicher, pp. 247-62. Boulder.

Ellen, R. F. 1987. Environmental Perturbation, Inter-Island Trade, and the Relocation of Production along the Banda Arc; or, Why Central Places Remain Central. Human Ecology of Health and Survival in Asia and the South Pacific, eds. T. Suzuki and R. Ohtsuka, pp. 35-61. Tokyo.

Ensminger, A. H., et al. 1994. Foods and Nutrition Encyclopedia. London.

Ermans, A. M., P. Bourdoux, J. Kinthaert, R. Lagasse, K. Luvivila, M. Mafuta, C. H. Thilly, and F. Delange. 1982. Role of Cassava in the Etiology of Endemic Goitre and Cretinism. Cassava Toxicity and Thyroid: Research and Public Health Issues, eds. F. Delange and R. Ahluwalia. Proceedings of a workshop held in Ottawa, 31 May-2 June. Ottawa.

Ermans, A. M., N. M. Mbulamoko, F. Delange, and R. Ahluwalia (eds.). 1980. Role of Cassava in the Etiology of Endemic Goitre and Cretinism. Ottawa.

Farb, P., and G. Armelagos. 1980. Consuming Passions: The Anthropology of Eating. New York.

Fernández de Oviedo, G. 1535. Historia natural y general de las Indias. By Royal Privilege.

Finney, B. 1973. Big Men and Business. Canberra.

—— 1987. Business Development in the Highlands of Papua New Guinea. Pacific Islands Development Program Series No. 6. Honolulu.

Food and Agriculture Organization. 1989a. Utilization of Tropical Foods: Roots and Tubers. Rome.

—— 1989b. Utilization of Tropical Foods: Trees. Rome.

Ford, E. 1959. Coffee Faces a Challenge. South Pacific 10:73-74.

Foster, G. M. 1994. Hippocrates' Latin American Legacy: Humoral Medicine in the New World. Langhorne PA.

Fox, J. J. 1991. The Heritage of Traditional Agriculture in Eastern Indonesia: Lexical Evidence and the Indications of Rituals from the Outer Arc of the Lesser Sunda Islands. Indo-Pacific Prehistory Association Bulletin 10:248-62.

Frechione, J. 1982. Manioc Monozoning in Yekuana Agriculture. Antropológica (Caracas, Venezuela) 58:53-74.

—— 1990. Supervillage Formation in the Amazonian Terra Firme: The Case of Asenöña. Ethnology 29(2):117-33.

Freeman, S. T. 1999. Plumbing the Pimiento Relleno: The Meaning of a Dish. Radcliffe Culinary Times 9(1):1, 8-10.

Galaty, J. G. 1982. Being "Maasai," Being "People of Cattle": Ethnic Shifters in East Africa. American Ethnologist 9(1):1-20.

Geertz, C. 1963. Agricultural Involution: The Process of Ecological Change in Indonesia. Berkeley.

Gillin, J. P. 1947. Moche: A Peruvian Coastal Community. Smithsonian Institution, Institute of Social Anthropology Publication no. 3. Washington DC.

Golson, J. 1982. The Ipomoean Revolution Revisited: Society and the Sweet Potato in the Upper Wahgi Valley. Inequality in New Guinea Highlands Societies, ed. A. Strathern, pp. 109-36. Cambridge.

Goodman, J. 1993. Tobacco in History: The Cultures of Dependence. London.

Gordon, R. 1992. The Bushman Myth: The Makings of a Namibian Underclass. Boulder.

Grenand, F. 1993. Bitter Manioc in the Lowlands of Tropical America: From Myth to Commercialization. Tropical Forests, People and Food: Biocultural Interactions and Applications to Development, eds. C. M. Hladik, A. Hladik, O. F. Linares, H. Pagezy, A. Semple, and M. Hadley, pp. 447-62. Paris.

Grossman, L. S. 1984. Peasants, Subsistence Ecology, and Development in the Highlands of Papua New Guinea. Princeton.

Gundel, K. 1993 (1934). Gundel's Hungarian Cookbook. Budapest.

Guss, D. M. 1989. To Weave and Sing: Art, Symbol, and Narrative in the South American Rain Forest. Berkeley.

Haddon, A. C. 1946. Smoking and Tobacco Pipes in New Guinea. Philosophical Transactions, Series B, 232. London.

Hall, R. L. 1991. Savoring Africa in the New World. Seeds of Change: A Quincentennial Commemoration, eds. H. J. Viola and C. Margolis, pp. 160-71. Washington DC.

Hanley, G. 1971. Warriors and Strangers. London.

Hansen, A., and D. E. McMillan (eds.). 1986. Food in Sub-Saharan Africa. Boulder.

Harlan, J. 1989. The Tropical African Cereals. Foraging and Farming: The Evolution of Plant Exploitation, eds. D. R. Harris and G. C. Hillman, pp. 335-43. London.

Harvey, P. W. J., and P. F. Heywood. 1983. Nutrition and Growth in Simbu. Research Report of Simbu Land Use Project, Vol. 4. Boroko.

Hassan, R. M., and D. D. Karanja. 1997. Increasing Maize Production in Kenya: Technology, Institutions, and Policy. Africa's Emerging Maize Revolution, eds. D. Byerlee and C. K. Eicher, pp. 81-93. Boulder.

Hather, J., and P. V. Kirch. 1991. Prehistoric Sweet Potato (*Ipomoea batatas*) from Mangaia Island, Central Polynesia. Antiquity 65:887-93.

Hays, T. E. 1991a. "No Tobacco, No Hallelujah": Missions and the Early History of Tobacco in Eastern Papua. Pacific Studies 14(4):91-112.

———— (ed.) 1991b. Encyclopedia of World Cultures: Vol. 2, Oceania. Boston.

Headland, T. N. 1997. Revisionism in Ecological Anthropology. Current Anthropology 38(4):605-30.

Heath, G. R. 1913. Notes on Miskito Grammar and on Other Indian Languages of Eastern Nicaragua. American Anthropologist 15:48-62.

Hecht, S. 1992. The Logics of Livestock and Deforestation: The Case of Amazonia. Development or Destruction? The Conversion of Tropical

Forest to Pasture in Latin America, eds. T. E. Downing, S. B. Hecht, H. A. Pearson, and C. Garcia-Downing, pp. 7-25. Boulder.

Helms, M. W. 1971. Asang: Adaptations to Culture Contact in a Miskito Community. Gainesville.

Henry, D. 1771. The Practical Farmer *or* The Complete English Farmer. London.

Hernsheim, E. 1983. South Sea Merchant, eds. and transl. P. Sack and D. Clark. Boroko.

Hicks, D., and M. A. Gwynne. 1996. Cultural Anthropology. New York.

Hinde, S. 1901. The Last of the Masai. London.

Hockings, P. (ed.) 1993. Encyclopedia of World Cultures: Vol. 5, East and Southeast Asia. Boston.

Holtzman, J. D. 1996. Transformations in Samburu Domestic Economy. Ph.D. dissertation, University of Michigan. Ann Arbor.

———— 1997. Gender and the Market in the Organization of Agriculture among Samburu Pastoralists in Northern Kenya. Research in Economic Anthropology 18:93-112.

Howlett, D., et al. 1976. Chimbu: Issues in Development. Deveopment Studies Centre No. 4. Canberra.

Hugh-Jones, C. 1979. From the Milk River: Spatial and Temporal Processes in Northwest Amazonia. Cambridge.

Hughes, H. I. 1978. Good Money and Bad: Inflation and Devaluation in the Colonial Process. Mankind 11:308-18.

Jackson, F. L. C. 1993. The Influence of Dietary Cyanogenic Glycosides from Cassava on Human Metabolic Biology and Microevolution. Tropical Forests, People and Food: Biocultural Interactions and Applications to Development, eds. C. M. Hladik, A. Hladik, O. F. Linares, H. Pagezy, A. Semple, and M. Hadley, pp. 321-38. Paris.

Jenness, D., and A. Ballantyne. 1920. The Northern D'Entrecasteaux. Oxford.

Johns, T. 1996. The Origins of Human Diet and Medicine. Tucson.

Johnston, H. H. 1886. The Kilim-Njaro Expedition. London.

Jones, W. O. 1959. Manioc in Africa. Stanford.

Kaneva-Johnson, M. 1995. The Melting Pot: Balkan Food and Cookery. Devon.

Karp, I. 1980. Beer Drinking and Social Experience in an African Society: An Essay in Formal Sociology. Explorations in African Systems of Thought, eds. I. Karp and C. S. Bird, pp. 83-119. Bloomington.

Kipkorir, B. E., and J. W. Ssenyonga. 1985. Sociocultural Profile of Elgeyo-Marakwet District. Nairobi.

Kirch, P. V. 1991. Prehistoric Exchange in Western Melanesia. Annual Review of Anthropology 20:141-65.

Kirchoff, P. 1948. The Caribbean Lowland Tribes: The Mosquito, Sumo, Paya, and Jicaque. Handbook of South American Indians, Vol. 4, ed. J. Steward, pp. 219-29. Washington DC.

Kocher-Schmid, C. 1994. Nur eine handvoll samen: zur Geschichte des Tabaks in Neuguinea. Traverse 1:111-21.

Korugl-Kumugl. 1998. Chimbu Coffee Faces Tough Times, Says BCIC. National. November.

Kuimbakul, T. 1994. Coffee Report No. 34. Coffee Industry Corporation Ltd. Port Moresby.

Lang, G. 1971. The Cuisine of Hungary. New York.

Lathrap, D. W. 1970. The Upper Amazon. New York.

Lentz, C. 1992. Migración e identidad étnica: La transformación histórica de una comunidad indígena en la sierra ecuatoriana. Quito.

——— 1997. Buscando la vida: Trabajadores temporales en una plantación de azúcar. Quito.

Lévi-Strauss, C. 1973. From Honey to Ashes, transl. J. Weightman and D. Weightman. London.

Lewis, L. A., and L. Berry. 1988. African Environments and Resources. Boston.

Little, P. D., and M. M. Horowitz. 1987. Subsistence Crops Are Cash Crops: Some Comments with Reference to Eastern Africa. Human Organization 46(2):254-58.

Long-Solís, J. 1998 (1986). Capsicum y cultura: La historia del chilli. México.

MacGregor, W. 1892. Despatch Reporting Administrative Visits to Tagula and Murua, &c. Annual Report on British New Guinea from 1st July, 1890, to 30th June, 1891, App. I., pp. 31-32.

——— 1894. Despatch Reporting Visit to Various Islands at the Eastern End of the Possession. Annual Report on British New Guinea from 1st July, 1892, to 30th June, 1983, App. B, pp. 3-7.

Macrae, R., et al. (eds.) 1993. Encyclopedia of Food Science, Food Technology and Nutrition. London.

Manglesdorf, P. C., R. S. McNeish, and G. R. Willey. 1964. Origins of Agriculture in Middle America. Handbook of Middle American Indians, Vol. 1: Natural Environment and Early Cultures, ed. R. C. West, pp. 427-45. Austin.

Marshall, M. 1981. Tobacco. Historical Dictionary of Oceania, eds. R. D. Craig and F. P. King, pp. 288-89. Westport.

——— 1991. The Second Fatal Impact: Cigarette Smoking, Chronic Disease, and the Epidemiological Transition in Oceania. Social Science and Medicine 33:1327-42.

Martyr de Angleria, P. 1966 (1490-1525). Letter 134. Opera: Legato Babylonica, De Orbe Novo Decades Octo, Opus Epistolarum. Graz.

Marx, W. G., and G. R. Heath. 1983. Diccionario: Miskito-Español, Español-Miskito. Winston-Salem.

Mason, J. A. 1973 (1940). The Native Languages of Middle America. The Maya and Their Neighbors, eds. C. L. Hay, R. L. Linton, S. K. Lothrop, H. L. Shapiro, and G. C. Valiant, pp. 52-87. New York.

Mathiesen, J. 1993. The Children of Lucanica. Petits Propos Culinaires 43:62-63.

Matson, G. A., and J. Swanson. 1963. Distribution of Hereditary Blood Antigens among Indians in Middle America (V. In Nicaragua). American Journal of Physical Anthropology 21:545-59.

McCormick, E. J., and W. K. Roberts. 1952. Paired Comparison Ratings II: The Reliability of Ratings Based on Partial Pairings. Journal of Applied Psychology 36(3):188-92.

Merker, M. 1910. Die Masai. Berlin.

Mintz, S. W. 1985. Sweetness and Power: The Place of Sugar in Modern History. New York.

—— 1987. Author's Rejoinder. Food and Foodways 2:171-97.

—— 1996. Tasting Food, Tasting Freedom: Excursions into Eating, Culture, and the Past. Boston.

Miracle, M. P. 1966. Maize in Tropical Africa. Madison.

Monk, K. A., et al. 1997. The Ecology of Nusa Tenggara and Maluku. Singapore.

Munnull, J. P., and D. R. Densley. n.d. Coffee. Agriculture in the Economy. Port Moresby.

Naj, A. 1993 (1992). Peppers: A Story of Hot Pursuits. New York.

Nelson, H. 1976. Black, White and Gold: Goldmining in Papua New Guinea 1878-1930. Canberra.

Nelson Sutherland, C. H. 1986. Plantas Comunes de Honduras, Vols. 1-2. Tegucigalpa.

Netting, R. M. 1964. Beer as a Locus of Value among the West African Kofyar. American Anthropologist 66(1):375-84.

Nietschmann, B. 1973. Between Land and Water: The Subsistence Ecology of the Miskito Indians, Eastern Nicaragua. New York.

Onwueme, I. C. 1978. The Tropical Tuber Crops. New York.

Orlove, B. 1982. Tomar la Bandera: Politics and Punch in Southern Peru. Ethnos 3-4:249-61.

Overland, D. 1998. An Investigation of the Household Economy: Coffee Production and Gender Relations in PNG. The Journal of Development Studies 34:52-70.

Padmaja, G. 1996. The Culprit in Cassava Toxicity: Cyanogens or Low Protein? CGIAR News 3(3):http://www.worldbank.org/html/cgiar/newsletter/Oct96/6cassava.htm].

Piperno, D. R., and D. M. Pearsall. 1998. The Origins of Agriculture in the Lowland Neotropics. San Diego.

Prinz, A. 1993. Ash Salt, Cassava and Goitre: Change in the Diet and the Development of Endemic Goitre among the Azande in Central Africa. Tropical Forests, People and Food: Biocultural Interactions and Applications to Development, eds. C. M. Hladik, A. Hladik, O. F. Linares, H. Pagezy, A. Semple, and M. Hadley, pp. 339-48. Paris.

Purseglove, J. W. 1968. Tropical Crops: Dicotyledons, Vols. 1, 2. New York.

―――― 1972. Tropical Crops: Monocotyledons, Vol. 1. New York.

Rambo, K. 1993. Economic Change and Differentiation in Kerowagi (Papua New Guinea). Ph.D. dissertation, State University of New York. Stony Brook.

Rand McNally and Company. 1994. The New International Atlas. Chicago.

Rekdal, O. B. 1996. Money, Milk and Sorghum Beer: Change and Continuity among the Iraqw of Tanzania. Africa 66(3):367-85.

Riebsame, W. E. 1990. The United States and Great Plains. The Earth as Transformed by Human Action: Global and Regional Changes in the Biosphere over the Past 300 Years, eds. B. L. Turner, II, W. C. Clark, R. W. Kates, J. F. Richards, J. T. Matthews, and W. B. Meyer, pp. 561-75. New York.

Riesenfeld, A. 1951. Tobacco in New Guinea and the Other Areas of Melanesia. Journal of the Royal Anthropological Institute 81:69-102, map.

Ríos, A., and L. March. 1992. The Heritage of Spanish Cooking. New York.

Roberts, B. D. 1993. The Historical and Ecological Bases of Economic Opportunity and Inequality in Elgeyo-Marakwet District, Kenya. Ph.D. dissertation, University of Pittsburgh.

―――― In Press. Always Cheaply Pleasant: Beer as a Commodity in a Rural Kenyan Society. Rethinking Commodities: Anthropological Views of the Global Marketplace, eds. P. Stone, A. Haugerud, and P. Little. Lanham MD.

Root, W. 1980. Food: An Authoritative and Visual History and Dictionary of the Foods of the World. New York.

Rouse, J. E. 1977. The Criollo: Spanish Cattle in the Americas. Norman.

Saka, A. R., W. T. Bunderson, O. A. Itimu, H. S. K. Phombeya, and Y. Mbekeani. 1994. The Effects of Acacia Albida on Soils and Maize Grain Yields under Smallholder Farm Conditions in Malawi. Forest Ecology and Management 64:217-30.

Salaman, R. N. 1949. The History and Social Influence of the Potato. Cambridge.

Sangree, W. H. 1962. The Social Functions of Beer Drinking in Bantu Tiriki. Society, Culture, and Drinking Patterns, eds. D. J. Pittman and C. R. Snyder, pp. 6-21. Carbondale.

Sauer, C. O. 1950. Cultivated Plants of South and Central America. Handbook of South American Indians, Vol. 6, ed. J. Steward, pp. 487-543. Washington DC.

———— 1969. Agricultural Origins and Dispersals: The Domestication of Animals and Foodstuffs. Cambridge MA.

———— 1992. The Early Spanish Main. Berkeley.

Scaglion, R., and K. A. Soto. 1994. A Prehistoric Introduction of the Sweet Potato in New Guinea? Migration and Transformations: Regional Perspectives on New Guinea, eds. A. Strathern and G. Stürzenhofecker, pp. 257-94. Pittsburgh.

Sexton, L. 1986. Mothers of Money, Daughters of Coffee: The *Wok Meri* Movement. Ann Arbor.

Shineberg, D. 1967. They Came for Sandalwood: A Study of the Sandalwood Trade in the South-West Pacific 1830-1865. Carlton.

Shipton, P. 1990. African Famines and Food Security: Anthropological Perspectives. Annual Review of Anthropology 19:353-94.

Simons-Gérard, E., P. Bourdoux, A. Hanson, M. Mafuta, R. Lagasse, L. Ramioul, and F. Delange. 1980. Foods Consumed and Endemic Goitre in Ubangi. Role of Cassava in the Etiology of Endemic Goitre and Cretinism, eds. A. M. Ermans, N. M. Mbulamoko, F. Delange, and R. Ahluwalia, pp. 69-80. Ottawa.

Simoons, F. J. 1991. Food in China: A Cultural and Historical Inquiry. Boca Raton.

Sinclair, J. 1995. The Money Tree. Bathurst.

Smith, A. F. 1994. The Tomato in America. Early History, Culture, and Cookery. Columbia.

Smith, N. J. H., J. T. Williams, D. L. Plucknett, and J. P. Talbot. 1992. Tropical Forests and Their Crops. Ithaca.

Sobania, N. 1991. Feasts, Famines and Friends: Nineteenth Century Exchange and Ethnicity in the Eastern Lake Turkana Region. Herders, Warriors and Traders: Pastoralism in Africa, eds. J. Galaty and P. Bonte, pp. 118-42. Boulder.

Spencer, P. 1965. The Samburu. Oxford.

Steward, J. H. 1948. The Circum-Caribbean Tribes: An Introduction. Handbook of South American Indians, Vol. 4, ed. J. Steward, pp. 1-41. Washington DC.

Steward, J. H., and L. C. Faron. 1959. Native Peoples of South America. New York.

Stone, D. (ed.) 1984. Pre-Columbian Plant Migration. Cambridge.

Stone, O. C. 1880. A Few Months in New Guinea. London.

Swadling, P. 1986. Papua New Guinea's Prehistory: An Introduction. Port Moresby.

Szathmary, L. 1992. Paprika: The Gift of Columbus to the Hungarian Kitchen. Paper presented to the Oxford Symposium on Food and Cookery, 12-13 September.

Terrón, E. 1992. España, encrucijada de culturas alimentarias: Su papel en la difusión de los cultivos americanos. Madrid.

Thompson, R. W. 1900. My Trip in the "John Williams." London.

Thomson, B. H. 1889. New Guinea: Narrative of an Exploring Expedition to the Louisiade and D'Entrecasteaux Islands. Royal Geographical Society, Proceedings, N.S., 11:525-42, map.

Thomson, J. 1885. Through Masailand. London.

Toussaint-Samat, M. 1992. History of Food, transl. A. Bell. Cambridge.

Turner, B. L., G. Hyden, and R. Kates (eds.). 1993. Population Growth and Agricultural Change in Africa. Gainesville.

Turner, W. Y. 1878. The Ethnology of the Motu. Journal of the Royal Anthropological Institute 7:470-99.

van Bath, B. H. S. 1966. The Agrarian History of Western Europe, A.D. 500-1850, transl. O. Ordish. London.

Viola, H. J., and C. Margolis (eds.). 1991. Seeds of Change: A Quincentennial Commemoration. Washington DC.

W., M. 1732. The Mosqueto Indian and His Golden River; Being a Familiar Description of the Mosqueto Kingdom in America, with a Relation of the Strange Customs, Religion, Wares, etc., of those Heathenish People. A Collection of Voyages and Travels, Vol. 6, ed. A. Churchill, pp. 285-98. London.

Ward, A. 1929. The Encyclopedia of Food. New York.

Warry, W. 1987. Chuave Politics. Changing Patterns of Leadership in the Papua New Guinea Highlands. Political and Social Change Monograph 4. Canberra.

Watson, J. B. 1965. From Hunting to Horticulture in the New Guinea Highlands. Ethnology 4:295-309.

―――― 1977. Pigs, Fodder, and the Jones Effect on Postipomoean New Guinea. Ethnology 16:57-70.

Weatherford, J. 1988. Indian Givers: How the Indians of the Americas Transformed the World. New York.

Weismantel, M. 1988. Food, Gender and Poverty in the Ecuadorian Andes. Philadelphia.

Weiss, E., with R. Buchan. 1983 (1979). The Paprikàs Weiss Hungarian Cookbook. New York.

Wiessner, P., and A. Tumu. 1998. Historical Vines: Enga Networks of Exchange, Ritual and Warfare in Papua New Guinea. Washington DC.

Wilkes, G. 1989. Maize: Domestication, Racial Evolution, and Spread. Foraging and Farming: The Evolution of Plant Domestication, eds. D. R. Harris and G. C. Hillman, pp. 440-55. London.

Willey, G. R. 1966. An Introduction to American Archaeology, Vols. 1-2. Englewood Cliffs.

Williams, L. O. 1981. The Useful Plants of Central America. Ceiba 24(1-2):1-342.

Wohlt, P. B., and A. Goie. 1986. North Simbu Land Use. Research Report of the Simbu Land Use Project, Vol. 5. Boroko.

Yen, D. E. 1974. The Sweet Potato and Oceania: An Essay in Ethnobotany. Honolulu.

Young, M. W. 1977. Bursting with Laughter: Obscenity, Values and Sexual Control in a Massim Society. Canberra Anthropology 1(1):75-87.

Young, T. 1971 (1847). Narrative of a Residence on the Mosquito Shore. New York.